The Everyday Chef

PICNICS
AND BARBECUES

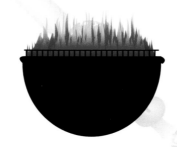

Published by Celebrity Press
Nashville, Tennessee 37218

Printed and bound in the United States of America

ISBN 1-58029-012-4

10 9 8 7 6 5 4 3 2 1

Graphic Design/Art Direction
John Laughlin

Contents

Conversion Table

Metric Conversions

1/8 teaspoon = .05 ml
1/4 teaspoon = 1 ml
1/2 teaspoon = 2 ml
1 teaspoon = 5 ml
1 tablespoon = 3 teaspoons = 15 ml
1/8 cup = 1 fluid ounce = 30 ml
1/4 cup = 2 fluid ounces = 60 ml
1/3 cup = 3 fluid ounces = 90 ml
1/2 cup = 4 fluid ounces = 120 ml
2/3 cup = 5 fluid ounces = 150 ml

3/4 cup = 6 fluid ounces = 180 ml
1 cup = 8 fluid ounces = 240 ml
2 cups = 1 pint = 480 ml
2 pints = 1 liter
1 quart = 1 liter
1/2 inch = 1.25 centimeters
1 inch = 2.5 centimeters
1 ounce = 30 grams
1 pound = 0.5 kilogram

Oven Temperatures

Fahrenheit	Celsius
250°F	120°C
275°F	140°C
300°F	150°C
325°F	160°C
350°F	180°C
375°F	190°C
400°F	200°C
425°F	220°C
450°F	230°C

Baking Dish Sizes

American	Metric
8-inch round baking dish	20-centimeter dish
9-inch round baking dish	23-centimeter dish
11 x 7 x 2-inch baking dish	28 x 18 x 4-centimeter dish
12 x 8 x 2-inch baking dish	30 x 19 x 5-centimeter dish
9 x 5 x 3-inch baking dish	23 x 13 x 6-centimeter dish
1 1/2-quart casserole	1.5-liter casserole
2-quart casserole	2-liter casserole

Beef

Al dente:

An Italian term meaning "firm to the teeth."

Blue Cheese:

A rich, blue-veined cheese, similar to Roquefort.

Brandon's Devilish Short Ribs

1/3 c spicy brown mustard
1/4 c prepared white horseradish
3 tbsp Worcestershire sauce
4 lb beef chuck short ribs, cut into
   serving-sized pieces
unseasoned meat tenderizer

In small bowl, mix mustard, horseradish, and Worcestershire sauce. Sprinkle ribs with meat tenderizer as label directs. Place ribs on grill over medium heat. Cook 30 minutes for medium-rare or to desired doneness, turning ribs often. Brush ribs frequently with mustard mixture during last 10 minutes of cooking.

Veggie Steak Kabobs

1 boneless beef sirloin steak (2 1/2 lb),
   cut into 1-inch chunks
1/4 c soy sauce
1/4 c dry sherry
2 tbsp vinegar
1 tbsp sesame oil
1/2 tsp ground ginger
1 large red onion
1 large sweet green pepper, stem and
   seeds removed, cut into large pieces
vegetable oil or cooking spray
olive oil

In medium-sized bowl, combine beef, soy sauce, vinegar, sugar, sesame oil, and ginger. Refrigerate beef 30 minutes to marinate.

Meanwhile, heat coals. Lightly oil grill rack or coat with cooking spray; set aside.

In heavy 2-quart saucepan, heat 2 inches water and onion to boiling over high heat; cook onion 5 minutes or until softened. Blanch pepper pieces a few seconds in same boiling water with onion. Drain vegetables. Cut onion into 12 wedge-shaped slices, keeping pieces intact.

Heat grill rack. On each of 6 long metal skewers, alternately thread vegetables with 3 chunks beef, reserving marinade. Brush vegetables with olive oil.

Place kabobs on hot grill rack about 4 inches above medium-hot coals. Grill 8 minutes or to desired doneness, turning and basting occasionally with reserved marinade.

Porterhouse Steak with Grilled Salad

1/4 c chili sauce
1/4 c balsamic vinegar
3/4 tsp salt
1 garlic clove, crushed
1 porterhouse steak, about 2 1/4 lb
   and 2 inches thick
Grilled Salad (recipe follows)

In a deep dish, mix chili sauce, vinegar, salt, and garlic. Trim all fat from steak; add steak to chili sauce mixture to coat.

Place steak on grill over medium heat and brush with half the chili sauce mixture remaining in baking dish. Cook steak 20 to 30 minutes for medium-rare or to desired doneness, turning steak occasionally and brushing with chili sauce mixture. Serve with Grilled Salad.
(*continued on page7*)

Grilled Salad

1 large head radicchio
3 medium heads Belgian endive
3 tbsp olive oil
1 tbsp dried rosemary
1/2 tsp salt

About 15 minutes before serving, cut radicchio into 6 wedges. Cut each head Belgian endive lengthwise in half. In small bowl, mix olive oil, rosemary, and salt. Place radicchio and endive on grill over medium heat; brush with olive oil mixture. Cook 5 to 10 minutes, turning occasionally, until vegetables are tender-crisp.

Chili Grilled Steaks

2 tsp chili powder
1 tsp paprika
3/4 tsp ground cumin
1/2 tsp salt
1/4 tsp black pepper, freshly ground
1/8 tsp ground red pepper
1 porterhouse steak (about 2 lb and 1 1/2 inches thick)
1 tbsp olive oil
1 large red bell pepper, quartered and seeded
1 large red onion, cut into 1/2-inch slices

Mix chili powder, paprika, cumin, salt, black pepper, and ground red pepper. Set aside 1 teaspoon. Sprinkle steak with remaining spice rub. Let steak sit at room temperature 1 hour. Prepare a hot fire in a charcoal or gas grill. In a small bowl, combine reserved spice rub and oil; brush onto pepper and onion. Grill steak 6 to 8 minutes per side for medium-rare or to desired doneness, turning once. Grill peppers and onions until tender, about 3 minutes per side, turning once. Let steak stand 5 minutes before slicing. Cut peppers into 1-inch strips. Serve sliced steak with onion and pepper.

Spice-Rubbed Beef Tenderloin

1 tbsp fennel seeds, crushed
2 tsp salt
1/2 tsp ground ginger
1/2 tsp red pepper, crushed
1 beef tenderloin roast (about 2 1/2 lb)

On waxed paper, combine fennel seeds, salt, ginger, and crushed red pepper. Rub spice mixture onto beef tenderloin. If desired, place spice-rubbed beef tenderloin in a plastic bag and refrigerate several hours or overnight before grilling.

Place beef in covered grill over medium heat. Cook covered, turning occasionally, 30 to 40 minutes for medium-rare or to desired doneness. Temperature on meat thermometer should be 135°F. (Internal temperature will go up to 140°F upon standing.)

Remove beef tenderloin to cutting board. Slice beef thinly to serve.

Hickory-Smoke Barbecued Steak

2 top sirloin steaks (about 8-oz each)
1/3 c barbecue sauce
4 drops hickory-smoke flavoring
1/2 tsp seasoned pepper
1 clove garlic, finely minced
1/4 c red wine

Mix all ingredients well in large baking dish. Marinade steaks in mixture for 60 to 90 minutes, then place on hot barbecue grill. Grill to desired doneness.

Stuffed Hamburgers

1 1/2 lb ground chuck
2 tbsp onion, finely chopped
hamburger dill pickle chips
4 tbsp blue cheese, crumbled
garlic powder
salt and pepper
4 Kaiser rolls or hamburger buns

Mix ground chuck and onion. Form mixture into 8 thin patties.

Arrange 4 to 6 pickle chips on each of 4 patties; top each with one tablespoon blue cheese and a second patty. Pinch edges of patties together to seal and form 4 hamburgers. Sprinkle with garlic powder, salt, and pepper. Broil or grill 12 minutes or until no longer pink and juices run clear. Serve on toasted Kaiser rolls or hamburger buns.

Steak Fajitas

1 skirt or flank steak (about 1 1/2-lb),
    sliced into 1 1/2-inch strips
1/4 c vegetable oil
1/4 c dark soy sauce
juice and zest of two limes
2 tbsp peppered vinegar
1 clove garlic, minced
1 tbsp chili powder

Place steak in a glass utility dish. Combine all remaining ingredients except chili powder; pour mixture over steak. Sprinkle steak with chili powder. Cover and refrigerate overnight.

Thread meat onto skewers and grill until medium-rare. Serve on folded tortillas with salsa, sour cream, and guacamole.

Beer-Basted Steaks

6 sirloin steaks
1/4 c brown sugar
1 1/2 tbsp mustard
1 tbsp white vinegar
1 onion, finely chopped
1 bay leaf
1 c beer

Combine all ingredients except steaks in a pan; bring to a boil. Reduce heat and simmer for 10 minutes; cool. Remove bay leaf. Pour mixture over steaks. Let stand 1 to 2 hours, turning steaks occasionally. Barbecue steaks until golden brown on both sides.

Grilled Leg of Lamb

1 lamb leg (about 3 lb), boneless and butterflied
3 garlic cloves, halved and crushed
2 tsp fennel seeds
2 tsp cumin seeds
2 tsp coriander seeds
1 tbsp olive oil
1 1/2 tsp salt
lemon wedges

Rub lamb with cut side of garlic cloves; discard garlic. Crush fennel, cumin, and coriander seeds. In small bowl, combine crushed seeds with olive oil and salt. With hand, rub lamb with crushed seed mixture.

Place lamb on grill over medium heat. Cook 15 to 25 minutes for medium-rare or to desired doneness, turning lamb occasionally. Thickness of butterflied lamb will vary throughout; cut off sections of lamb as they are cooked and place on cutting board. Serve with lemon wedges.

Grilled Mustard Pepper Steak

1/2 c dry red wine
1/2 c vegetable oil
2 shallots, minced
1 small clove garlic, minced
1/4 c grainy mustard
2 tbsp Worcestershire sauce
2 tbsp coarsely cracked peppercorns
1 tsp dried thyme
salt and red pepper sauce to taste
6 steaks, such as strip or rib-eye

Combine wine, oil, shallots, garlic, 2 teaspoons mustard, Worcestershire sauce, 1/2 teaspoon peppercorns, thyme, and salt in a blender or food processor; mix well. Transfer to a glass baking dish and add steaks, turning several times so they are well coated. Cover and refrigerate 4 hours or overnight, turning several times.

Prepare a medium-hot charcoal fire. Combine remaining mustard and hot pepper sauce in a small dish.

Remove steaks from marinade; pat dry. Spread a thin layer of mustard mixture over one side of each steak and add some of remaining peppercorns.

Place steaks on grill, mustard-side down. Brush with remaining mustard; sprinkle with pepper. Grill about 6 inches from coals, turning once, 8 to 12 minutes for medium-rare or to desired doneness.

Extra-Special Burgers

1 lb ground beef
1/4 tsp salt
1/4 tsp garlic salt
1/8 tsp pepper
1 tbsp soy sauce
1 jar (2 1/2 oz) mushroom pieces, drained
3/4 c cheddar cheese, grated
6 slices bacon, fried and crumbled
1 tbsp dried parsley

Thoroughly combine ground beef, salt, garlic salt, pepper, and soy sauce. Divide mixture into 8 thin patties.

Combine remaining ingredients; divide evenly atop 4 patties. Place another patty on top of each; seal edges.

Refrigerate until ready to cook. Cook on grill or under broiler to desired doneness.

VARIATIONS:

Reuben Burger
Stuff with 1 cup shredded Swiss cheese combined with 6 tablespoons well drained sauerkraut.

Blue Cheese Burgers
Stuff with 1/2 cup crumbled blue cheese, 1/4 cup sour cream, and 1/4 cup drained sweet pickle cubes.

Almost Filet Mignon with Mushroom Sauce

1 lb ground beef
1 tbsp vegetable oil
1 clove garlic, minced
1 tsp salt
1/2 tsp pepper
4 strips bacon
Mushroom Sauce (recipe follows)

Combine meat, oil, garlic, salt, and pepper. Mix well. Shape into 4 patties. Wrap each patty with bacon; fasten with toothpicks. Cook on grill 10 to 15 minutes on each side or to desired doneness. Serve with Mushroom Sauce.

Mushroom Sauce

3 tbsp butter
1 tbsp Worcestershire sauce
1 dash red pepper sauce
1/4 tsp seasoned pepper
1 can (4 oz) mushroom pieces, drained

Melt butter and add seasonings. Sauté mushrooms in seasoned butter. Serve with grilled patties.

Green Chili Burgers

1 1/2 lb ground beef
1 clove garlic, crushed
1 dash pepper
1 tsp ground chili
1/2 tsp salt
1/2 c Monterey Jack cheese, shredded
4 hamburger buns
4 green chilies, parched and chopped
4 slices red onion
1 medium tomato, sliced
4 leaves romaine or red lettuce
fresh salsa

Mix beef with garlic, pepper, ground chili, and salt in a large bowl. Shape into 4 flat patties. Preheat broiler or grill. Cook burgers to desired doneness. Just before serving, sprinkle cheese on top of each bun. Toast buns until lightly browned and cheese is melted. Top each bun with a hamburger patty, green chilies, onion slice, tomato slice, and lettuce leaf. Serve immediately with fresh salsa on the side.

French Burgers

1 1/2 lb ground beef
2 tsp grape jelly
1/8 tsp cayenne pepper
2 oz Brie or Camembert, cut into 6 slices
1 1/2 tsp onion powder
1 tsp dried thyme
1/2 tsp garlic powder
1/4 tsp salt
1/4 tsp black pepper

Mix grape jelly and cayenne into beef. Shape beef into 12 oval patties, each about 1/2-inch thick.

Center a slice of cheese on 6 of patties. Top those 6 patties with remaining plain patties, crimping edges together to seal.

Combine onion powder, thyme, garlic powder, salt, and pepper. Sprinkle both sides of each burger with about 1/2 teaspoon spice mixture; pat firmly into meat.

Place patties on grill over hot coals; cook to desired doneness.

Pork

Chop:
To cut into small, irregular-shaped pieces.

Combine:
To stir together two or more ingredients.

Kim's Teriyaki Pork Chops

2 green onions, chopped
1/3 c soy sauce
2 tbsp ginger root, grated and peeled
2 tbsp plus 1/4 c packed light brown sugar
4 pork loin chops, each 3/4-inch thick
1 small pineapple
green onion strips for garnish

In 13x9-inch glass baking dish mix green onions, soy sauce, ginger, and 2 tablespoons brown sugar.

Add pork chops, turning to coat with teriyaki mixture. Let stand 20 minutes to marinate.

Meanwhile, cut rind from pineapple, then cut pineapple crosswise into half-inch slices. Rub pineapple slices with 1/4 cup brown sugar.

Place pineapple slices on grill over medium heat. Cook pineapple slices 15 to 20 minutes until browned on both sides, turning slices occasionally. After pineapple has cooked 10 minutes, add pork chops.

Cook until lightly browned on both sides and chops just lose their pink color throughout, about 10 minutes. Turn chops occasionally and brush with remaining teriyaki mixture halfway through cooking time.

Serve pork chops with grilled pineapple slices. Garnish with green onion strips.

Honey Pork Chops

4 pork chops
3 tbsp clear honey
3 tbsp chopped marjoram
3 tbsp chopped thyme
salt and pepper
juice of half a lemon

Brush chops on both sides with honey. (If honey is thick, warm slightly to thin.) Mix chopped herbs and coat chops with them evenly. Sprinkle with salt, pepper, and lemon juice. Grill for 5 minutes on each side, close to heat, then another 5 to 10 minutes on each side, depending on thickness, further away from heat. Serve immediately.

Caribbean Grill

4 pork chops, each about 1 1/2-inches thick
1 large red onion, sliced
3/4 c lime juice
1/2 tsp cayenne pepper

Arrange pork in a single layer in a non-reactive pan or dish. Combine remaining ingredients in a bowl and pour over pork, turning pork to coat. Cover and marinate in refrigerator for at least 3 hours.

Prepare medium-hot coals in covered grill, banking coals on sides of grill. Remove chops from marinade, reserving marinade. Grill chops over indirect heat 15-18 minutes, turning once. Heat marinade to boiling; serve with pork.

Plum-Glazed Pork Kabobs

1 pork tenderloin (about 1 1/2-lb)
1 red onion, cut into 12 wedges
1 to 2 bell peppers, cut into 12 squares
1/3 c plum jelly or jam
2 tbsp soy sauce
1/2 tsp ground ginger
1 clove garlic, minced

Trim all visible fat from meat. Cut meat into 12 cubes. Thread onto skewers, alternating with onion wedges and pepper squares. Combine remaining ingredients in 1-cup glass measure. Microwave on high for 1 minute; stir to blend. Place kabobs on grill over medium-hot fire. Grill until browned, about 10 to 12 minutes, turning and basting frequently with glaze.

Spicy Barbecued Sandwiches

1 pork roast (about 5 lb)
2-inch piece ginger root
3 cloves garlic
1 bunch green onions, white part only
3/4 c soy sauce
1 c bottled Hoisin sauce
1/3 c Asian sesame oil
3/4 c honey
1 c ketchup
1/3 c unseasoned rice vinegar

Wash roast and trim any fat. Set aside. Process ginger root, garlic, and green onions until minced. Add soy sauce and process again. Pour this and remaining ingredients into a medium saucepan and heat gently for 20 minutes. Pour over roast and let marinate in refrigerator for 24 to 48 hours.

Remove roast, reserving marinade. Grill roast over hot wood or hardwood charcoal, adding more to keep heat as roast cooks. This will take approximately 2 to 3 hours, depending on grill and type of fuel used. When finished, remove roast and let cool.

Meanwhile, bring marinade to a boil. Reduce heat and boil gently for 10 minutes. Reserve for later use. Shred pork and blend with barbecue sauce.

Pork Spareribs with Tomato Barbecue Sauce

1 pork rib
salt and pepper to taste
Tomato Barbecue Sauce (see below)

Season pork ribs with salt and pepper. Barbecue ribs on coals until done. Remove ribs from coals and quickly apply Tomato Barbecue Sauce with a barbecue brush, covering whole rib on both sides. Return ribs to coals and continue barbecueing each side for 2 minutes only. Remove, cut, and serve.

Tomato Barbecue Sauce
1 c ketchup
1/2 c sugar
1/2 c vinegar

Combine all ingredients. Mix well.

Tomato Barbeque Sauce should be applied to ribs after they have been barbecued to perfection, and each treated side barbecued for only 2 minutes more after applying sauce.

Citrus-Barbecued Pork Chops

3/4 c barbecue sauce
1/4 c orange juice
1 tsp grated orange peel
1/2 tsp dried rosemary leaves, crushed
1/2 tsp dried thyme leaves, crushed
4 pork loin chops, each about 1-inch
  thick (about 2 lb)

Place all ingredients except chops in saucepan; bring to boil. Reduce heat to low and simmer for 10 minutes, stirring occasionally.

Heat grill. Place chops on greased grill over medium coals; brush generously with barbecue sauce mixture. Cover and grill 15 minutes. Turn; brush with barbecue sauce mixture. Continue grilling, covered, 10 to 15 minutes or until cooked through. Makes 4 servings.

Orange Barbecued Ribs

1 c barbecue sauce
1/4 c orange juice
1 tsp grated orange peel
1/2 to 1 tsp crushed red pepper flakes
3 lb pork spareribs or backribs

Mix barbecue sauce, juice, peel, and pepper. Heat grill. Place ribs, bone side down, on greased grill over low coals. Grill, uncovered, 30 minutes on each side. Brush with barbecue sauce mixture; continue grilling 30 minutes or until done, turning and brushing with barbecue sauce mixture every 10 minutes.

OVEN METHOD: Heat oven to 350°F. Place ribs on rack of broiler pan. Brush with barbecue sauce mixture. Bake 1 hour and 15 minutes or until done, turning and brushing with barbecue sauce mixture every 15 minutes.

Grilled Pork Skewers

2 green mangoes
1/2 tbsp crushed red pepper flakes
1/4 c pineapple juice
1/2 tbsp white vinegar
1/8 tsp turmeric
1/8 tsp ground cumin
1/8 tsp curry powder
1/8 tsp chili powder
1 tbsp minced garlic
1 lb pork tenderloin, trimmed of fat and
  cut into 1-inch cubes
1 red bell pepper, seeded and cut into
  1-inch squares
1/2 to 1 large red onion, cut into chunks
salt and pepper to taste

Make marinade by peeling one green mango and slicing fruit away from pit. Purée fruit in a blender or food processor with pepper flakes, pineapple juice, vinegar, turmeric, cumin, curry powder, chili powder, and garlic. Pour marinade over pork cubes; cover and refrigerate for about 4 hours.

Peel second mango and cut fruit away from pit; cut mango into 1-inch cubes. Remove meat from marinade, leaving as much marinade as possible on pork cubes.

Thread pork cubes and pieces of mango, red pepper, and onion onto 8-inch skewers. Season with salt and pepper. Grill over medium heat until pork is cooked, about 5-7 minutes per side.

Poultry & Game Hens

Baguette:
A long, narrow loaf of French bread.

Kabobs
Small pieces of meat or seafood seasoned or marinated and broiled, often with vegetables, usually on a skewer.

All-American Barbecued Chicken

2 tbsp olive oil
1 large onion, chopped
2 cans (15 oz each) tomato sauce
1 c red wine vinegar
1/2 c light molasses
1/4 c Worcestershire sauce
1/3 c packed brown sugar
3/4 tsp ground red pepper
2 chickens (3 1/2 lb each), quartered
   and skin removed, if desired

In 10-inch skillet, heat olive oil over medium heat. Add onion and cook until tender, about 10 minutes. Stir in tomato sauce, vinegar, molasses, Worcestershire sauce, brown sugar, and ground red pepper; heat to boiling over high heat.

Reduce heat to medium-low and cook, uncovered, 45 minutes or until sauce thickens slightly.

Reserve 1 1/2 cups sauce to serve with grilled chicken. Place chicken quarters on grill over medium heat; cook 20 to 25 minutes, turning once. Generously brush chicken with some of remaining barbecue sauce.

Cook 20 minutes longer, turning pieces often and brushing with sauce frequently. Chicken is done when juices run clear when chicken is pierced with tip of knife. Serve with reserved sauce.

Grilled Citrus Turkey Cutlets with Cucumber Sauce

1 pkg turkey breast cutlets
1/3 c fresh lime juice
2 garlic cloves, minced
1/2 tsp curry powder
1/4 tsp ground cumin
1/4 tsp salt
1/4 tsp cayenne
pita bread

Spray unheated grill rack with cooking spray. Prepare grill for medium direct-heat cooking. Combine lime juice, garlic, curry powder, cumin, salt, and cayenne.

Dip cutlets in lime juice mixture. Place cutlets on rack over medium-hot grill. Turn once or twice for even cooking and browning.

Cook 5 to 7 minutes per side or until meat is no longer pink. Serve with cucumber sauce.

Cucumber Sauce
1 c plain yogurt
1/2 c cucumber, shredded
1 tsp lime peel, grated
1/2 tsp ground cumin
1/2 tsp salt

Combine yogurt, cucumber, lime peel, cumin, and salt. Chill.

Texas Turkey Kabobs

1 pkg turkey breast medallions (or chunks
  of raw turkey breast about 1-inch wide)
1/4 c vegetable oil
4 tbsp fresh lime juice
1 tsp chili powder
1/2 tsp garlic powder
1 1/2 tsp salt
2 medium yellow squash, cut into
  3/4-inch chunks
2 medium onions, cut into 3/4-inch chunks
2 red bell peppers, cut into 3/4-inch chunks
2 green bell peppers, cut into 3/4-inch chunks

Spray unheated grill rack with cooking spray.
Prepare grill for medium direct-heat cooking.

Combine oil, lime juice, chili powder, garlic
powder, and salt. Place vegetables in oil mixture
and stir to coat. Remove vegetables.

Add turkey medallions to oil mixture and stir to
coat. Thread turkey and vegetables alternately
onto skewers, leaving a small space between
pieces.

Place kabobs on rack over medium-hot grill.
Baste with remaining oil mixture during
cooking.

Turn frequently for even cooking and browning.

Cook for 25 to 30 minutes or until meat is no
longer pink.

Grilled Turkey with Black Bean Salsa

1 pkg turkey breast cutlets
1 tbsp chili powder
1 tsp salt

Spray unheated grill rack with cooking spray.
Prepare grill for medium direct-heat cooking.

Combine chili powder and salt and sprinkle over
both sides of cutlets. Place cutlets on rack over
medium-hot grill.

Turn two to three times for even cooking and
browning. Cook 5 to 7 minutes per side or until
meat is no longer pink.

Serve with chilled Black Bean Salsa.

Black Bean Salsa
1 can (15 oz) black beans, drained and rinsed
1 can (11 oz) Mexicorn, drained
1 c fresh tomatoes, diced
2 tbsp green onions, sliced
1 tsp garlic, minced
2 tbsp cilantro
4 tsp lime juice
4 tsp olive oil
salt and pepper

Combine black beans, corn, tomatoes, green
onions, garlic, and cilantro into a large bowl.
Pour lime juice and olive oil into bowl; stir to
blend. Add salt and pepper to taste. Chill.

Caribbean Turkey Grill

1 pkg turkey breast tenderloins
2 tbsp peach preserves
4 green onions
4 cloves garlic
1 tsp red pepper sauce
1/4 tsp black pepper
1 tsp salt
2 tbsp lime juice
1 tsp lime peel, shredded
1 1/2 tsp soy sauce

Spray unheated grill rack with cooking spray. Prepare grill for medium direct-heat cooking.

In food processor or blender, purée all ingredients except turkey. Spread turkey tenderloins with purée and place on rack over medium-hot grill. Cook tenderloins for about 20 minutes or until meat is no longer pink, turning frequently for even cooking and browning.

Oven-Barbecued Chicken

2 lb chicken parts
1 can (10 3/4-oz) tomato soup
1/4 c vinegar
1/4 c vegetable oil
2 tbsp packed brown sugar
1 tbsp Worcestershire sauce
1 tsp garlic powder
1/8 tsp Louisiana-style hot sauce (optional)

Place chicken in 2-quart shallow baking dish and bake at 375°F for 30 minutes. Spoon off fat.

Mix soup, oil, vinegar, sugar, Worcestershire sauce, garlic powder, and hot sauce. Spoon over chicken. Bake 30 minutes more or until chicken is no longer pink. Remove chicken. Stir sauce.

Grilled Pita Chicken

3 boneless and skinless chicken breasts, cut into 1-inch chunks
1/3 c creamy peanut butter
2/3 c lite coconut milk
1/4 c honey
3 tbsp soy sauce
1-inch piece ginger root
2 sweet onions, quartered
2 bell peppers, chunked
4 pita pockets, halved

Place chicken in a bowl and set aside.

Blend peanut butter, coconut milk, honey, soy sauce, and ginger root until smooth.

Pour over chicken pieces and marinate overnight.

The next day, light grill 30 to 60 minutes before mealtime.

Skewer chicken pieces separately from vegetables.

Cook chicken 7 minutes on one side; turn and cook other side an additional 6 minutes.

Place vegetable skewers on grill 10 minutes before chicken is done.

Serve chicken and some grilled onion and peppers in pita pockets.

Barbecue Ranch Chicken Salad

1/2 c barbecue sauce
1 lb boneless and skinless chicken breast
  halves, cut into strips
1 pkg (10 oz) mixed salad greens
1 c mushrooms, sliced
1 c pitted ripe olives
1/2 c red onion, sliced
1/2 c Ranch dressing
1/4 c blue cheese, crumbled
tortilla chips, coarsely crushed

Heat barbecue sauce in skillet on medium-high heat. Add chicken; cook and stir until chicken is cooked through. Add additional barbecue sauce, if desired.

Toss greens, mushrooms, olives, and onion in large bowl. Top with chicken. Pour dressing over greens mixture. Sprinkle with cheese and crushed chips.

Tangy Grilled Chicken Kabobs

1 c salad dressing
1 pkg dry Italian-style salad dressing mix
2 tbsp vinegar
2 tbsp water
1 1/2 lb boneless and skinless chicken breast
  halves, cut into 1 1/2-inch pieces
assorted fresh vegetables (peppers, mushrooms,
  onions, zucchini), cut into pieces.

Mix dressing, dressing mix, vinegar, and water to blend. Reserve 1/2 cup dressing mixture. Arrange chicken and vegetables on 6 skewers. Marinate 30 minutes in dressing mixture. Place kabobs on grill over medium-high coals; brush with additional dressing mixture.

Grill 10 to 15 minutes or until chicken is cooked through, turning once. Makes 6 servings.

Chicken Breast Teriyaki

1/4 c soy sauce
1 tsp crushed ginger root
1/4 c sweet white wine
1 clove garlic
1 tbsp sugar
1 1/2 lb chicken breast fillets
1 tbsp vegetable oil

Mix all ingredients, adding chicken last. Refrigerate for no less than 60 minutes. Grill chicken, basting with remaining marinade.

Chicken in Chimichurri Sauce

1 c curly parsley leaves
1 c olive oil
1 tbsp lemon juice
1 tsp cracked black peppercorns
6 cloves garlic
1/2 tsp salt
1 lb boneless and skinless chicken breast
  meat, cut into 1-inch-wide strips

Put all ingredients except chicken into blender or food processor and blend until smooth. Put half of the sauce into a glass bowl or plastic food bag. Add chicken; turn to coat well. Marinate in refrigerator for 1 to 4 hours. Refrigerate other half of sauce.

Preheat grill. If using wooden skewers, soak them in water at least 20 minutes to prevent burning.

Thread chicken onto skewers. Grill chicken, basting occasionally with sauce, until chicken is no longer pink and edges are slightly golden, 10 to 15 minutes. Serve immediately with refrigerated sauce for dipping.

Chicken Fajitas

2 tbsp oil
1 1/2 lb boneless and skinless chicken
   breasts and thighs, cut into thin slices
1 large onion, slivered from pole to pole
1 green bell pepper, slivered from pole to pole
1 red bell pepper, slivered from pole to pole
4 cloves garlic, finely chopped
2 tbsp chili powder
3 tsp ground cumin
1 tsp black pepper
salt and ground red pepper to taste
flour tortillas

Warm oil in a large wok. Cook chicken slices until done, stirring regularly. Add all remaining ingredients except tortillas; mix well. Cook covered, stirring every few minutes, until peppers are tender and vegetables are starting to get browned in spots. Serve with warmed flour tortillas.

Suggested additional fajita toppings: salsa, sour cream, avocados, tomatoes.

Bangkok Barbecued Chicken with Sweet and Spicy Dipping Sauce

2 frying chickens (3 1/2 lb each), split in half
1 can (14 oz) unsweetened coconut milk
1 tbsp curry powder
2 tbsp Thai fish sauce
6 cloves garlic, coarsely chopped
1/3 c cilantro, loosely packed and chopped,
   stems included
2 1/2 tbsp golden brown sugar
1/2 tbsp white pepper
Sweet and Spicy Dipping Sauce
(recipe follows)

Place chicken halves skin side up in a shallow roasting pan. Lightly score chicken to allow marinade to penetrate. Set aside.

Combine coconut milk, curry powder, fish sauce, garlic, cilantro, sugar, and pepper in a blender. Blend until smooth. Pour marinade over chicken halves, then turn them skin side down. Spoon some of marinade into chicken cavities.

Marinate in refrigerator at least 3 hours or overnight, turning occasionally to coat each half. Preheat grill. Arrange chicken halves on grill and cook for about 30 minutes or until juices run clear when leg joint is pierced with a fork. Turn chicken occasionally and baste frequently with marinade.

Transfer chicken to a cutting board and chop into serving pieces. (Each chicken half can yield 5 pieces.) Arrange chicken pieces on a large serving platter and serve hot, warm, or at room temperature with dipping sauce.

Sweet and Spicy Dipping Sauce

1/2 c distilled white vinegar
1 c sugar
1/2 tsp salt
1 tbsp Chinese-style chili-garlic sauce

In a small sauce pan, combine vinegar and 1/2 cup of sugar. Bring to a low boil over medium-high heat, stirring occasionally. Lower heat to medium and stir in rest of sugar. Cook for 2 minutes, stirring frequently as mixture comes to a boil. Reduce heat to low and add salt. Simmer for 5 minutes, stirring occasionally. Stir in chili-garlic sauce and remove from heat. Let cook and serve at room temperature. This sauce will keep for 2 to 3 weeks if kept covered and refrigerated.

Chicken Breasts with Spicy Rub

4 chicken breasts
2 tsp vegetable oil

Spicy Rub
2 tbsp ground cumin
2 tbsp paprika
2 tbsp brown sugar
1 tbsp black pepper
1 tsp curry powder
1 tsp cayenne
1 tsp salt
1 tbsp Dijon mustard
1 tbsp red wine vinegar
1 tbsp vegetable oil
2 cloves garlic, minced

Pat chicken breasts dry. Combine ingredients for rub. Smear rub over both sides of chicken, adding rub as desired to make chicken spicier. Brush grill with 2 tablespoons oil. Place chicken on grill skin side down.

Cook over medium heat 10 to 12 minutes per side until chicken is just cooked through. (If heat is too high, coating will burn; if too low, cooking time will be a little longer).

Spanish Mixed Grill

1/4 c red wine vinegar
1 tsp salt
1/2 tsp coarsely ground black pepper
3 tbsp olive oil
2 tbsp fresh oregano leaves, chopped
8 large skinless chicken thighs
3 medium red onions
3/4 lb *chorizo*, each fully cooked and
  cut crosswise in half
2/3 c olives

In large bowl, combine vinegar, salt, pepper, 2 tablespoons olive oil, and 1 tablespoon chopped oregano; add chicken thighs, tossing to coat.

Refrigerate 30 minutes to marinate. Meanwhile, cut each red onion into 6 wedges; thread onto 3 metal skewers.

Place red onion skewers on grill over medium heat; brush with 1 tablespoon olive oil. Cook 5 minutes.

Place chicken thighs on grill with onions; cook about 20 minutes, turning onions and chicken once, until onions are browned and tender and juices run clear when chicken thighs are pierced with the tip of a knife.

About 10 minutes before onions and chicken are done, add *chorizo* pieces to grill and cook, turning occasionally, until lightly browned and heated through.

To serve, place red onion skewers on platter with chicken and *chorizo*.

Sprinkle with remaining chopped oregano.

Serve with olives.

Mixed Grill

1/2 c orange marmalade
2 tbsp lemon juice
1 tbsp fresh rosemary, chopped
3/4 tsp salt
6 frankfurters, fully cooked
1 chicken (about 4 lb), quartered
tomato wedges for garnish

In small bowl, mix orange marmalade, lemon juice, rosemary, and salt. Cut a few slashes in each frankfurter to prevent them from bursting while cooking.

Place chicken quarters on grill over medium heat; cook until golden on both sides, about 10 minutes. Stand chicken pieces upright, leaning one against the other, to avoid charring. Rearrange pieces from time to time while cooking. Cook until fork-tender and juices run clear when pierced with knife, about 25 minutes longer. During last 10 minutes of cooking, place frankfurters on same grill. Brush chicken quarters and frankfurters frequently with orange marmalade mixture.

Grilled Jalapeño-Turkey Burgers

1 pkg all-white turkey, ground
1/4 c green onions, chopped
1 clove garlic, minced
1 tsp Worcestershire sauce
2 tbsp pickled jalapeño, chopped
1/2 tsp salt
1/8 tsp ground black pepper

Lightly spray unheated outdoor grill rack with cooking spray. Prepare grill for medium direct-heat cooking.

Combine ground turkey, green onions, garlic, Worcestershire sauce, jalapeño, salt, and pepper. Combine mixture and form into 6 large patties. Place patties on rack over medium-hot grill. Turn 2 to 3 times for even cooking and browning. Cook 6 minutes per side or until meat is no longer pink. Serve with your favorite condiments.

Barbecued Quail

6 quail
1 bottle dry white wine
3 fresh sage leaves
1 sprig fresh rosemary
juice of 2 lemons
12 strips bacon
olive oil for basting
salt and freshly ground pepper to taste

Prepare marinade by combining wine, sage, and rosemary in a large baking dish.

Place quails in marinade and cover; refrigerate overnight. Turn birds once.

Prepare barbecue grill. Remove birds from marinade. Rub birds both inside and outside with lemon juice. Tie two strips of bacon together and around each bird.

Place two birds on each skewer. Grill birds, turning frequently, until tender and browned. Baste with olive oil. Season with salt and pepper to taste.

Roast Cornish Hen with Lemon

12 imported black olives, pitted
1 small sprig fresh rosemary, leaves only
6 sprigs Italian parsley, minced
4 tbsp extra-virgin olive oil
salt and pepper
2 Cornish hens, split
2 lemons, seeded and thinly sliced

Preheat oven to 400°F.

In a small bowl, mash together olives, rosemary, parsley, and olive oil using a mortar and pestle or the tines of a fork. Set aside.

Rinse hens in cool water and pat dry with paper towels. Gently slip an index finger under skin on thigh and on breast, separating skin from bird as much as possible without tearing fragile skin. Slide a layer of thinly sliced lemons under skin of both breast and thigh.

Rub outside of each bird with olive-rosemary mixture. Lightly season birds with salt and pepper. Place on an oiled rack set in a shallow roasting pan. Place in preheated oven and roast for 45 to 60 minutes or until done. Remove and cool completely before refrigerating.

Barbecued Duck Aloha

2 ducklings, (about 4 lb each)
salt and pepper
1/2 c onion, chopped
1/2 c celery, chopped
1 apple, chopped
1/4 c sherry
1/4 c soy sauce
1/2 tsp ground ginger
2 tbsp lemon juice

Preheat grill. Season ducklings with salt and pepper. Fill cavities with a mixture of onions, celery, and apple.

Clip off wing tips. Run spit lengthwise through birds, catching each bird in the fork of its wishbone.

Cook on a rotisserie until tender (about 2 hours). Brush with a mixture of sherry, soy sauce, ginger, and lemon juice during last half hour of cooking.

This recipe also works well with Cornish game hens, quail, and dove.

Grilled Chicken Burgers

4 chicken breasts, minced
3 tbsp butter
1 c red pepper, chopped fine
6 shallots, minced
2 c bread crumbs
2 eggs, beaten
1/2 c cream or milk
2 tbsp Dijon mustard
2 tbsp fresh herbs, minced
salt and pepper to taste

Mix all ingredients together. Chill for at least 1 hour or as long as overnight. Shape chicken mixture into large patties.

Place on a piece of greased aluminum foil or in a greased grill basket. Grill over medium-high heat until done, about 5-8 minutes per side, depending on thickness.

Cilantro Grilled Turkey Breast

2 tbsp soy sauce
3 tbsp rice wine or white vinegar
2 tbsp lime or lemon juice
1 tbsp lime or lemon zest
1 tbsp sesame oil
3 tbsp peanut oil
1 tbsp brown sugar
1/2 tsp cilantro
1/2 c coriander leaves
1 turkey breast, deboned

Combine first 9 ingredients to make marinade. Marinate turkey breast for at least 1 hour. Drain turkey breast and roll up into a bundle, using butcher's twine to keep it together. Grill over medium-high heat, turning often, until done, about 8-10 minutes per side.

Grilled Chicken Salad

1 1/2 c Italian salad dressing
2 tbsp honey
1 1/2 tbsp prepared mustard
4 boneless and skinless chicken
   breast halves (about 1 1/4 lb)
2 small zucchini, halved lengthwise
2 small red bell peppers, quartered
6 c assorted salad greens

Blend Italian dressing, honey, and mustard. Refrigerate 1/2 cup of marinade for salad greens and 1/2 cup for brushing.

In large, shallow, nonreactive baking dish or plastic bag, pour remaining marinade over chicken, zucchini, and peppers; turn to coat. Cover dish or close bag, and marinate in refrigerator, turning occasionally, up to 3 hours.

Remove chicken, zucchini, and peppers from marinade, discarding marinade. Grill or broil chicken and vegetables, turning and brushing frequently with 1/2 cup refrigerated marinade, until chicken is done.

Meanwhile, toss salad greens with remaining 1/2 cup refrigerated marinade. Evenly divide salad greens on 4 plates. Slice and arrange 1 chicken breast on top of each salad. Cut vegetables and divide equally onto greens.

Sticky Wings

24 chicken wings (about 4 lb)
3/4 c Italian salad dressing
1 c peach preserves
1 tbsp hot pepper sauce (optional)

Cut tips off chicken wings. Cut chicken wings in half at joint.

Blend Italian dressing, preserves, and hot pepper sauce. In large, shallow, nonreactive baking dish or plastic bag, pour half of marinade over chicken wings; toss to coat. Cover dish or close bag, and marinate in refrigerator for at least 3 hours and up to 24 hours, turning occasionally. Refrigerate remaining marinade.

Remove wings, discarding marinade. Grill or broil wings until done, turning once and brushing frequently with refrigerated marinade.

Seafood

Cube:
To cut into uniform-sized pieces that are about
1/2-inch on each side.

Dice:
To cut into uniform-sized pieces
1/8- to 1/4-inch on each side.

Squash and Shrimp Kabobs

24 extra-large shrimp (about 1 1/2 lb),
  shells removed, deveined, tails attached
2 tbsp extra-virgin olive oil
2 tsp Worcestershire sauce
1/2 tsp pepper
1/4 tsp salt
dash red pepper sauce
1 medium-sized zucchini, trimmed and
  cut into half-inch slices
1 medium-sized yellow squash, trimmed
  and cut into half-inch slices

In large bowl, combine shrimp, oil,
Worcestershire sauce, seasoned pepper, salt,
and pepper sauce until well mixed. Refrigerate
30 minutes to marinate.

Meanwhile, in heavy 4-quart saucepan, heat 2
inches water to boiling. Add zucchini and
squash; cook until tender-crisp (about 2
minutes). Drain vegetables and rinse with cold
water. Add vegetables to shrimp mixture and
toss until coated with seasonings.

Heat coals in grill until hot. Lightly oil or coat
grill rack with cooking spray and set aside.

Heat grill rack. Prepare kabobs: on each of 6
long metal skewers, alternately thread shrimp
and vegetables. Place kabobs on hot grill rack
about 3 inches above hot coals. Grill kabobs for
1 to 2 minutes per side or until shrimp are firm
and pink.

Shrimp Sonoma

1 oz dried tomatoes without salt
1 1/2 lb large shrimp
2 tbsp lemon juice
2 tbsp olive oil
1/2 tsp salt
1/2 tsp crushed red pepper

Place dried tomatoes in small bowl. Pour 1 cup
boiling water over tomatoes; let stand while
preparing shrimp.

Cut legs from shrimp by inserting tip of kitchen
shears under shell of each shrimp and snipping
along back to tail, cutting about a fourth of an
inch deep to expose dark vein. Leaving shell on,
rinse shrimp to remove vein. Place shrimp in
bowl.

Drain dried tomatoes, reserving 1/4 cup
soaking liquid.

In blender or in food processor with knife blade
attached, combine tomatoes with reserved
soaking liquid, lemon juice, olive oil, salt, and
pepper until well blended. Pour over shrimp.

On 4 long skewers, thread shrimp. Place
skewers on grill over medium heat.

Cook 8 to 10 minutes until shrimp turn opaque
throughout, turning skewers occasionally and
basting with any remaining tomato mixture.

Butter-Barbecued Salmon

1 whole salmon (about 6 to 8 lb), cleaned
salt and pepper
2 c mushrooms, chopped
1 c green onions, chopped
2 tbsp parsley minced
1/2 c Parmesan cheese, grated
grated peel and juice of 1 lemon
1/2 c (1 stick) butter or margarine, melted
4 to 5 lemon slices
Butter Sauce, Chili-Cheese Sauce, or
   Tartar Sauce (see below)

Remove head from salmon, if desired. Place salmon on double thickness of wide foil, making sure foil is 3 to 4 inches longer than fish at each end.

Sprinkle fish inside and out with salt and pepper to taste. Combine mushrooms, onion, parsley, cheese, lemon peel, and juice. Spoon mixture into fish cavity. Pour butter over fish and top with lemon slices. Cover with another thickness of foil and carefully seal all sides completely.

Place on grill 4 to 6 inches from glowing coals. Turn after 30 minutes and cook 20 to 30 minutes longer. If cooking on smoke-type grill, open foil during last 10 minutes and close grill cover so smoke flavor penetrates fish. Serve with choice of sauces.

Butter Sauce

1/2 c butter or margarine
1 c sour cream
1/4 tsp seasoned or onion salt
1 tsp chives, chopped

Melt butter in small saucepan over low heat. Stir in sour cream, seasoned salt, and chives. Warm, but do not boil.

Chili-Cheese Sauce

1/2 c butter or margarine
1/2 c chili sauce
1/3 c blue cheese, crumbled

Combine butter and chili sauce in small saucepan. Heat slowly until butter melts. Add cheese and keep warm until ready to serve.

Tartar Sauce

1/2 c butter or margarine
1 c sour cream
2 tbsp sweet pickle relish
1 envelope tartar sauce mix

Melt butter in small saucepan over low heat. Remove from heat and stir in remaining ingredients. Refrigerate.

Grilled Shrimp

2 lb large or jumbo shrimp, peeled and deveined
1/3 c olive oil
1/4 c tomato sauce or puréed tomatoes
2 tbsp red wine vinegar
2 tbsp fresh basil, chopped
1 clove garlic, minced
1/2 tsp salt
1/2 tsp cayenne pepper
vegetables such as garlic, red and/or yellow bell peppers, cherry tomatoes

In a bowl, stir together oil, tomato sauce, vinegar, basil, minced garlic, salt, and cayenne pepper. Add shrimp and toss to coat evenly. Cover and refrigerate for about two hours, stirring occasionally.

Put shrimp on skewers with vegetables. Cook on medium-hot grill for about 6 minutes, basting with leftover marinade.

Salmon with Dill and Caper Sauce

1/4 c drained capers, chopped
2 tbsp fresh dill, chopped
2 tbsp lemon juice
2 tsp sugar
2 tsp anchovy paste
1 salmon fillet, (about 2 lb)
1/4 tsp salt
fresh dill and lemon wedges for garnish

In small bowl, mix capers, dill, lemon juice, sugar, and anchovy paste. Remove any small bones from salmon fillet; sprinkle with salt. Place salmon in lightly greased fish basket; brush all caper sauce on flesh-side only.

Place fish basket on grill rack. Over medium heat, cook salmon 5 minutes on each side or until it flakes easily when tested with a fork. Garnish with fresh dill and lemon wedges.

Salmon Teriyaki

1 lb salmon
3 cloves garlic, pounded once to remove
    skins and finely chopped
2 tbsp soy sauce
1 tbsp honey
1 tsp parsley or cilantro
1 tsp red pepper flakes
1 tbsp vinegar or 1 tbsp lime juice
1 tbsp brown sugar

Wash and scale salmon under cold water. Slice into thin pieces. Mix garlic, soy sauce, honey, parsley, red pepper, and lime juice in a non-metallic bowl. Marinate salmon for 1 hour.

Heat grill to medium-high. Carefully lay salmon pieces on a sheet of tinfoil. Poke small holes in foil with a fork to let smoky flavor in. Sprinkle with approximately 1 tablespoon brown sugar. Grill until just crispy and edges are beginning to caramelize. Serve with white rice.

Grilled Crab With Blender Béarnaise

1/4 c white wine vinegar
1 1/2 tsp onion or chives, minced
1 tsp tarragon leaves, crushed
3 egg yolks
1 tsp Dijon mustard
1/4 tsp salt
1/4 tsp pepper
1 1/2 sticks (3/4 c) butter
1/4 c chopped ripe olives
2 lb Alaska king, Dungeness, or snow crab legs

In small, microwaveable bowl, combine vinegar, onion or chives, and tarragon. Microwave on high about 2 minutes or until vinegar is reduced to 2 tablespoons; set aside.

Place egg yolks, mustard, salt, and pepper in blender; blend on low speed for 3 seconds. Put butter in microwaveable cup and cover; microwave on high until melted, about 2 minutes. With blender on low, gradually pour hot butter into yolks in a steady stream; turn off blender. Add vinegar mixture and olives and blend until just combined. Keep warm.

Cook crab on hot grill for about 5 minutes.

Serve with sauce.

Sauces & Marinades

Purée
To convert a food into a liquid or heavy paste
with a blender or food processor.

Marinate:
To soak food in a seasoned liquid mixture
for a certain length of time.

Cherry Sauce

1 lb cherries, pitted and chopped
1/3 c yellow pepper, diced
1 green onion, chopped
2 tbsp seasoned rice vinegar
1 tsp ginger root, grated and peeled
1/8 tsp salt

Mix all ingredients in a medium-sized bowl, stirring gently to combine. Cover and refrigerate for at least 1 hour to blend flavors. May be refrigerated for up to 2 days. Makes about 3 cups.

Peach Sauce

1 3/4 lb ripe peaches, peeled, pitted,
 and coarsely chopped
2 tbsp red onion, finely chopped
1 tbsp fresh mint leaves, chopped
1 tbsp lime juice
1 tsp jalapeño, seeded and finely chopped
1/8 tsp salt

Mix all ingredients in a medium-sized bowl, stirring gently to combine. Cover and refrigerate for at least 1 hour to blend flavors. May be refrigerated for up to 2 days. Makes about 3 cups.

Tomato Sauce

1/2 tsp lime peel, grated
2 tbsp fresh lime juice
1 1/2 lb ripe tomatoes, diced
1/2 small red onion, diced
1 small jalapeño, seeded and finely diced
2 tbsp fresh cilantro, chopped
3/4 tsp salt
1/4 tsp coarsely ground black pepper

Mix lime peel and juice with remaining ingredients in a medium-sized bowl, stirring gently to combine. Cover and refrigerate for at least 1 hour to blend flavors.

May be refrigerated for up to 2 days.
Makes about 3 cups.

Plum Sauce

1 1/2 lb ripe plums, pitted and coarsely chopped
1 green onion, chopped
1 tbsp fresh basil, coarsely chopped
2 tbsp balsamic vinegar
1/8 tsp salt

Mix all ingredients in a medium-sized bowl, stirring gently to combine. Cover and refrigerate for at least 1 hour to blend flavors. May be refrigerated for up to 2 days. Makes about 3 cups.

Watermelon Sauce

1 watermelon (about 2 1/2 lb), seeds and
 rind removed and coarsely chopped
1 tbsp red onion, finely chopped
1 tbsp fresh cilantro, chopped
2 tbsp lime juice
2 tsp jalapeño, seeded and finely chopped
1/8 tsp salt

Mix all ingredients in a medium-sized bowl, stirring gently to combine. Cover and refrigerate for at least 1 hour to blend flavors. May be refrigerated for up to 2 days. Makes about 3 cups.

Crazy Chicken Marinade

2 c water
4 tsp salt
2 tsp pepper
1 clove garlic, minced
1 tsp yellow food coloring
juice and some zest of one lemon
1 tsp paprika

Mix ingredients well. Marinate chicken in refrigerator for at least 2 hours or overnight before grilling.

Spicy Hot Barbecue Sauce

This makes a nice dipping sauce for meat or lavishing on your sandwiches.

2 tbsp vegetable oil
2 large cloves garlic, minced
1 c ketchup
1/3 c red wine vinegar
1 medium onion, chopped
1 c dry red wine
1 tsp Worcestershire sauce
2 tbsp Hoisin sauce
1 tbsp hot chili paste
fresh lemon juice to taste
salt and pepper to taste

In medium saucepan, heat oil and sauté garlic until translucent. Add ketchup, vinegar, onion, red wine, Worcestershire sauce, Hoisin sauce and chili paste to sauce. Add lemon juice, salt, and pepper to taste.

Place saucepan over low heat and cover. Let sauce simmer for 1 to 2 hours to let flavors develop, stirring occasionally.

Marinade-Baste for Ribs and Chicken

2 c apple cider vinegar
1 c water
3 tbsp ground black pepper
2 tbsp salt
1 tbsp Worcestershire sauce
1 tbsp paprika
1 tbsp chili powder

Heat ingredients in saucepan and use warm for basting and short-term marinating. For overnight marinating, allow to cool before using.

Finishing Sauce for Ribs

1/4 c unrefined sugar
1/2 c tamarind
1/2 c banana
1/2 tsp ancho chili powder
1/2 tsp sea salt
1 clove garlic, minced
1/4 c sweet white vinegar
1 1/2 tsp red pepper sauce

Mix ingredients in blender or with whisk. Brush over ribs that are still warm from grill.

All-Purpose Barbecue Sauce

1/4 c salad oil
2 tbsp soy sauce
1/4 c bourbon, sherry, or wine
1 tsp garlic powder
1/2 tsp pepper, freshly ground

Combine all ingredients and pour over meat. Marinate meat in refrigerator. Use leftover marinade to baste meat while cooking. Good on red meat, fish, or chicken.

Orange Barbecue Sauce

6 oz chili sauce
1/4 c orange juice
1/4 c soy sauce
1/4 c molasses
2 tbsp Chinese black vinegar
2 tbsp onion, grated
1/2 tsp ginger, grated
2 tsp hot pepper sauce

Combine all ingredients in a large saucepan. Stir to blend. Bring to a boil and let cool. Makes about 1 1/4 cups. Will keep for a brief period if refrigerated. Serve with barbecued ribs, roast chicken, or beef.

Citrus Barbecue Sauce

1 large onion, finely chopped
1 tbsp ground red chili peppers
1/4 tsp ground red pepper
1 ancho chili, seeded and finely chopped
1 tbsp vegetable oil
1 c orange juice
1/2 c lime juice
2 tbsp sugar
2 tbsp lemon juice
1 tbsp cilantro, snipped
1 tsp salt

Cook onion, chili peppers, red pepper, and ancho chili in oil, stirring frequently, until onion is tender, about 5 minutes. Stir in remaining ingredients. Heat to boiling; reduce heat to low. Simmer uncovered, about 10 minutes, stirring occasionally. Makes about 2 1/3 cups.

Mustard Barbecue Sauce

1/2 c sugar
1/4 tsp ground oregano
1/2 tsp ground thyme
1 tsp salt
1/2 tsp pepper
1/8 tsp cayenne pepper
1/2 tsp cornstarch
1/2 c vinegar
1 c molasses
1 c ketchup
1 c prepared mustard
2 tbsp vegetable oil

Combine first seven ingredients in a small saucepan. Stir in enough vinegar to make a paste. Combine molasses, ketchup, mustard, oil, and remaining vinegar; add to herb paste. Bring to a boil, stirring constantly. Reduce heat and simmer 10 minutes. Remove from heat; cool completely.

Pour into a glass jar; cover tightly. Store refrigerated for up to 3 months. Use as a baste over chicken, turkey, ham, or hot dogs.

Dad's Barbecue Sauce

1/2 c canola oil
1/3 c apple cider vinegar
1/2 c ketchup
1/2 c orange juice
1/4 c onion, grated
1 jalapeño, finely chopped
1/4 tsp oregano
2 cloves garlic

Combine all ingredients except oil in blender. Blend until smooth. Place blended ingredients and oil in saucepan. Boil for 7 to 8 minutes.

World-Famous Barbecue Sauce

16 oz hot sauce
2 1/2 tsp crushed red pepper flakes
1 small onion, sliced
1 small stalk celery, sliced
3 c tomato purée
1 1/2 c water
1 1/2 c sugar
1 lemon, sliced

Combine all ingredients in a heavy pot and heat until just hot; do not boil. Cool to room temperature, strain and store refrigerated in a tightly covered jar. Makes 5 cups.

Spiced Barbecue Sauce

1 c ketchup
1 can (6 oz) tomato paste
1 1/2 c honey
1 1/2 tsp olive oil
2 tsp red pepper sauce
1 tsp cayenne pepper
1 tbsp Worcestershire sauce
1 tbsp cocoa powder
1 tsp lemon juice
1/2 tbsp soy sauce
1/2 tsp black pepper
1 1/2 tbsp curry powder
1 tbsp paprika
2 cloves garlic, crushed

Stir everything together and simmer for 20 minutes.

Barbecue Sauce Dijon

1/4 tsp powdered oregano
1/4 tsp powdered thyme
1/4 tsp ground black pepper
dash of cayenne pepper
1 c prepared mustard
2 tbsp Dijon mustard
1/4 c cider vinegar, divided
1/2 c molasses
1/4 c honey
1 tbsp corn oil

In a stainless steel saucepan, mix oregano, thyme, peppers, and mustard (including Dijon if using). Add half of cider vinegar and stir. Stir in rest of cider vinegar and remaining ingredients. Bring to a boil; reduce heat and simmer for 10 minutes, stirring continuously.

Garlic Barbecue Sauce

1 can (16 oz) no-salt tomato sauce
1 can (4 oz) sliced mushrooms
2 tbsp honey
1 clove garlic, chopped
1 tsp chili powder
1 tbsp basil
1 tbsp oregano

Mix well. Add to meat or chicken before cooking.

Blender Hollandaise

3 egg yolks
2 tbsp lemon juice
dash cayenne pepper
1/2 c butter

Place first 3 ingredients in blender; cover and process until just combined.

Heat butter until melted and almost boiling; with blender on low speed, slowly add melted butter through center opening in blender cover. Replace top and turn blender to high speed. Blend 30 seconds on high or until thick and fluffy, scraping sides of blender as needed. Serve immediately.

Pork Barbecue Sauce

16 oz tomato sauce
2 tbsp brown sugar
1/4 c vinegar
2 tbsp Worcestershire Sauce
1 tsp salt
1 tbsp paprika
1 tsp dry mustard
1 tsp chili powder
2 tbsp green onion tops, chopped
1/8 tsp cayenne pepper

Combine all ingredients and simmer for 15 minutes, stirring occasionally. Serve hot. Makes 2 1/2 cups.

Whiskey Barbecue Sauce

1/2 large onion, minced
4 cloves garlic, minced
3/4 c whiskey
2 c ketchup
1/3 c vinegar
1/4 c Worcestershire sauce
1/3 tsp hot red pepper sauce
3/4 c molasses
1/2 tsp black pepper
1/2 tbsp salt
1/4 c tomato paste
2 tbsp liquid smoke
1/2 c packed brown sugar

Combine onion, garlic, and whiskey in a large saucepan. Sauté until onion and garlic are translucent, about 8-10 minutes; remove from heat. Light mixture; let flame for 20 seconds before extinguishing. Add all remaining ingredients; bring to a boil. Simmer for 20 minutes, stirring constantly.

Barbecue Marinade

1/4 c fresh lemon juice
juice of 3 large limes
1 tbsp soy sauce
1 tsp red wine vinegar
1/2 c cilantro, chopped
2 cloves garlic, chopped
1/4 tsp salt
pepper to taste

Combine all ingredients in a large mixing bowl; pour over meat. Marinate meat in refrigerator for at least 1 hour before cooking.

Plano Barbecue Sauce

2 c tomato catsup
2 tbsp wine vinegar
2 tbsp soy sauce
1 tbsp brown sugar
dash of hot red pepper sauce

Combine all ingredients in saucepan. Bring to a boil over moderate heat, stirring constantly. Reduce heat and simmer for 10 minutes. Serve hot or cold.

Dipping Sauce For Barbecue Chicken

1/2 tsp dried chili flakes or cayenne
2 cloves garlic, chopped coarse
1 tbsp brown sugar
1/4 tsp salt
1/2 c Chinese red rice vinegar
1 green onion, sliced thin
1 tbsp cilantro leaves, coarse chopped

Pound first 4 ingredients into to a paste with mortar and pestle, then dissolve in vinegar. (Or combine first 4 ingredients in a blender and process until smooth.) Float green onion and cilantro on top.

Salads & Sides

Extra-Virgin Olive Oil:
Oil made from the first pressing of
highest quality olives.

Rotisserie:
A small broiler with a motor-driven spit,
for barbecuing fowl, beef, etc.

Picnic Potato Salad

5 lb potatoes
1/2 c celery, finely chopped
4 eggs, hard-boiled
1/2 c fresh parsley, finely chopped
1 c dill relish
3/4 c mayonnaise
1/2 c sweet relish
1/4 c prepared mustard
1 c olives, chopped
1 tsp salt (or more to taste)
1 c onions, finely chopped
1 tsp Louisiana-style hot sauce

Boil potatoes in their jackets. Let cool, then peel and chop into large chunks.

Mix mayonnaise, mustard, hot sauce, and salt. Add potatoes and remaining ingredients; mix well. This recipe may be made the day before and refrigerated overnight.

Add more mayonnaise if potato salad is dry after being refrigerated.

Southwestern-Style Salad

1 can (16 oz) red kidney beans, rinsed
   and drained
2 green onions with tops, thinly sliced
1 small red bell pepper, coarsely chopped
1 c Monterey Jack cheese, shredded
1/4 c cilantro, coarsely chopped
1/4 c prepared salsa or picante sauce
1/4 c bottled Italian dressing
1 tbsp fresh lime juice
1/2 tsp ground cumin
Romaine lettuce leaves
lime wedges for garnish if desired

Combine beans, green onions, bell pepper, cheese, and cilantro in large bowl. In another bowl combine salsa, dressing, lime juice, and ground cumin; mix well.

Add to bean mixture and toss. Serve on lettuce leaves and garnish with lime wedges. May be prepared up to one day in advance. Keep covered and chilled.

Grilled Sweet Corn

8 medium-sized ears of corn with husks
8 tsp olive oil
several sprigs each basil, rosemary, sage, and thyme

Into 8-quart Dutch oven or kettle, place corn with husks and enough water to cover; let soak 15 minutes. (Soaking unshucked corn in water keeps husks from burning on grill.)

Remove corn from water and drain well. Gently pull husks three-fourths way down; remove silk.

With pastry brush, brush each ear of corn with 1 teaspoon olive oil. Tuck several sprigs of herbs next to kernels.

Re-wrap corn with husks, removing 1 strip of husk from each ear of corn and tying tops of corn with removed strip.

Place corn on grill over medium heat; grill 30 to 40 minutes, turning corn occasionally, until tender. Makes 8 servings.

Grilled Potato and Sausage Salad

2 lb small red potatoes, halved
5 tbsp vegetable oil
1 bunch green onions
1 turkey kielbasa (about 1 lb)
5 tbsp apple cider vinegar
2 tbsp sugar
1 tbsp whole grain, Dijon-style
    prepared mustard
1 tbsp water
1/4 tsp salt
1/4 tsp ground black pepper

Preheat outdoor grill. Coat grill rack with cooking spray. In large bowl, toss potatoes with 1 tablespoon oil. Grill potatoes about 4 inches from medium-hot coals, turning occasionally, until well browned (about 20 minutes). Set aside bowl with any remaining oil. Transfer browned potatoes to large piece of heavy-duty aluminum foil; wrap and continue to grill potatoes over low coals until fork-tender — about 20 minutes longer. Trim roots off onions. Toss onions in bowl with reserved oil. Cut kielbasa into 4 links.

Grill kielbasa and onions over medium-low coals, turning frequently, until lightly browned (about 4 minutes). Transfer sausages and onions to cutting board. Cut kielbasa into quarter-inch thick slices. Cut grilled green onions into one-inch lengths and cut each potato half into 2 wedges.

Dressing

In jar with tight-fitting lid combine remaining 4 tablespoons oil, vinegar, sugar, mustard, water, salt, and pepper until well mixed. In large serving bowl, toss potatoes, kielbasa, and onions with dressing. Serve immediately.

Grilled Vegetables Vinaigrette

2 tbsp olive oil
2 tbsp white wine vinegar
2 tsp fresh tarragon, chopped
1/2 tsp salt
1/2 tsp coarsely ground black pepper
1/2 tsp sugar
vegetables for grilling (see choices below)
tarragon sprigs for garnish

In large bowl, mix all ingredients except vegetables and tarragon sprigs. Add vegetables and toss to coat with vinaigrette dressing.

Grilled Peppers

Cut 2 medium-sized yellow peppers and 2 medium-sized red peppers in half lengthwise; discard seeds.

Place peppers on grill over medium heat and cook, turning occasionally and brushing with vinaigrette until peppers are browned and tender when pierced with a fork. Serve with remaining vinaigrette. Garnish with fresh tarragon sprigs.

Grilled Zucchini

Slice each of 4 small zucchini (6 oz each) lengthwise in half. Toss in vinaigrette. Grill until tender.

Grilled Baby Eggplants

Slice each of 4 baby eggplants (4 oz each) lengthwise in half. Toss in vinaigrette. Grill until tender.

Grilled Portobello Mushrooms

Trim tough stem ends from 2 medium-sized portobello mushrooms (4 oz each) or 8 jumbo mushrooms. Rinse; pat dry. Toss mushrooms in vinaigrette. Grill until tender.

Grilled Aubergine with Peanut Sauce

1 large aubergine (eggplant)
3 tbsp olive oil
salt and freshly ground black pepper
Peanut Sauce (see below)

Slice aubergine and lay slices on grill. Brush each slice with olive oil and season with salt and pepper. Grill on both sides until cooked (around 10 minutes total). Serve with Peanut Sauce for dipping. Serves four.

Peanut Sauce

1 tbsp butter
1 clove garlic, crushed
2 shallots, finely chopped
2 oz warm water
2 tbsp soy sauce
5 tbsp smooth peanut butter
1 tsp grated ginger
hot chili sauce to taste

Melt butter in a saucepan; add shallots and garlic. Cook until soft but not brown. Pour in water, soy sauce, peanut butter, and ginger. Bring to a boil and season with hot chili sauce. Simmer until desired thickness is reached.

Pioneer Pasta Salad

6 oz wagonwheel pasta
5 all-beef hot dogs, boiled and sliced in rounds
1/3 c sweet pickle, thinly sliced
1/4 c red or green pepper, finely chopped
2 green onions, thinly sliced
1/2 c mayonnaise
1 tbsp prepared mustard
2 tsp apple cider vinegar
salt and pepper
parsley to garnish

Cook pasta according to package directions. Drain and rinse well with cold water. Place hot dogs and pasta in large bowl and add remaining ingredients. Toss gently. Refrigerate for at least 2 hours.

Note: This is a great pasta salad for picnics with lots of children.

Corn Salad

6 ears sweet corn
8 cherry tomatoes, halved
1/8 red onion, diced
1/4 red or green bell pepper, diced
1/2 small *jicama*, diced
1/2 bunch fresh cilantro, washed
juice of 2 limes
1 tsp ground cumin
1 tsp salt
1 tsp canned, mild green chilies, chopped
1/3 c olive oil

Remove kernels from ears of corn and lightly steam for 1 to 2 minutes. Rinse in cold water to stop cooking process. Drain well and place corn in a medium-sized bowl. Add tomatoes, red onion, bell pepper, and *jicama*.

In bowl of a food processor fitted with a steel blade, place cilantro, limes, cumin, salt, and chilies. Process until ingredients are blended and minced. With motor running, slowly pour in olive oil. Dressing will thicken. Stop machine and pour dressing over corn salad. Refrigerate until ready to serve.

Caesar Potato Salad

1 c Caesar salad dressing
10 c cooked potatoes, hot and sliced
1/2 c (2 oz) Parmesan cheese, grated
1/4 c fresh parsley, chopped
1/4 c roasted red peppers, chopped

Pour dressing over potatoes in large bowl. Add cheese, parsley, and peppers. Toss to mix well. Serve warm or chilled.

Bacon and Chive Potato Salad

6 c small red potatoes, unpeeled and quartered
3/4 c mayonnaise
2 tbsp stone ground mustard
8 slices bacon, crisply cooked and crumbled
1/4 to 1/2 c chives, chopped (or green onions, sliced)

Place potatoes in boiling water; cook 15 minutes or until tender. Drain. Mix mayonnaise and mustard in large bowl. Add potatoes, bacon, and chives or onions; mix lightly. Refrigerate.

Easy Baked Beans

1 tsp vegetable oil
1 medium onion, chopped
2 cans (16 oz each) baked beans
1/2 c coffee, brewed
1/4 c honey
1/2 tsp dry mustard
1/4 tsp ground pepper

Preheat oven to 350°F.

Heat oil in large skillet on medium heat. Add onion; cook and stir until tender. Pour beans into casserole or bean pot and add onion.

Mix remaining ingredients and pour over beans. Bake 45 to 60 minutes or until liquid is almost completely absorbed and top is crisp. Makes 4 cups.

Crunchy Bacon Coleslaw

3/4 c salad dressing
1 tbsp sugar
4 c green cabbage, shredded
1 c red cabbage, shredded
1/2 c peanuts, chopped
4 slices bacon, crisply cooked and crumbled

Mix dressing and sugar in large bowl. Add remaining ingredients; mix lightly. Refrigerate.

Ham 'n Cheese Coleslaw

2/3 c olive oil
1/4 c white wine vinegar
2 tbsp Dijon mustard
1 tsp dill weed
1 tsp dried thyme
1/2 tsp pepper
1 pkg (16 oz) shredded cabbage
12 oz baked or honey ham, cut into thin strips
2 c (8 oz) Swiss cheese
3 dill pickles, coarsely chopped
1/4 c onion, finely chopped
1/4 c parsley, chopped

Whisk dressing ingredients: olive oil, white wine vinegar, Dijon mustard, dill weed, thyme leaves, and pepper in large bowl until well blended.

Add salad ingredients: shredded coleslaw, baked or honey ham, Swiss cheese, pickles, onion, and parsley to bowl; stir well. Cover. Refrigerate 30 minutes or overnight. Makes 10 cups.

Roasted Potato Salad

4 c small red potatoes, quartered and unpeeled
1 c salad dressing
4 slices bacon, crisply cooked, chopped,
  and drained
2 eggs, hard-cooked and chopped
1/4 c green onions, sliced
1/4 tsp salt
1/4 tsp pepper

Preheat oven to 425°F. Place potatoes on
15x10x1-inch baking pan sprayed with cooking
spray. Bake 30 to 35 minutes or until potatoes
are tender and golden brown, stirring once.

Mix dressing, bacon, eggs, onions, salt, and
pepper in large bowl. Add potatoes; mix lightly.
Serve warm or chilled.

Great American Potato Salad

3/4 c mayonnaise
1 tbsp prepared or Dijon mustard
1 1/2 tsp celery seed
1/2 tsp salt
1/8 tsp pepper
4 c potatoes, cooked and cubed
2 eggs, hard-cooked and chopped
1/2 c onion, chopped
1/2 c celery, sliced
1/3 c dill pickle relish

Mix mayonnaise, mustard, and seasonings in
large bowl. Add remaining ingredients; mix
lightly. Refrigerate. Makes 6 servings.

Spicy Macaroni 'n Cheese

1 lb elbow macaroni, cooked
1 tbsp butter
1 tbsp flour
1 tbsp milk, warmed
1/2 tsp paprika
1/4 tsp cayenne pepper
2 c cheese (Cheddar, Monterey Jack, Gouda,
mozzarella, or mixed)

Melt butter in small saucepan over medium
heat. When it starts bubbling, mix in flour.
Continue mixing for about a minute. Slowly
mix in warmed milk. Bring to a boil, stirring
constantly, until mixture thickens. When thick,
stir in paprika, cayenne and half of cheese.
Remove from heat.

Lightly grease a 2 1/2-quart casserole dish. Pour
in half of macaroni and half of sauce. Repeat
and sprinkle with remaining cheese.

Bake at 350°F for 25 to 30 minutes or until top
is lightly browned.

Variations
1/2 kielbasa, thinly sliced (mix with cooked
macaroni) 1 bunch broccoli florets, steamed
(mix with cooked macaroni) 1 to 2 c croutons
(sprinkle on top) 3 to 6 oz green chilies (mix
with cooked macaroni)

Vegetable Pasta

1 1/2 lb fresh green beans, cut in
   1 1/2-inch pieces
1/2 lb fresh mushrooms, cleaned and sliced
1 onion, sliced
5 cloves garlic, minced
1/2 c red wine
1 can (32 oz) crushed tomatoes
2 tsp dried basil
1 tsp dried marjoram
1 lb pasta (any variety)
black pepper, freshly ground

Put wine in a large skillet or Dutch oven. Add all vegetables and herbs except tomatoes. Cover and let simmer for 10 to 15 minutes. Add crushed tomatoes. Let simmer 30 more minutes.

Cook pasta in water without salt or oil. Combine with vegetables and enjoy.

Pasta Mexicali

4 oz rigatoni, cooked and drained
3/4 c frozen corn
3/4 c kidney beans, cooked
1/2 c spaghetti sauce (any variety)
1/4 tsp chili powder
salt and pepper to taste

Combine all ingredients except pasta in a small saucepan; cook until everything is heated through. When done, add pasta and mix well.

Barcelona Tuna and Potato Salad

1 1/2 lb new red potatoes (about 5 c)
1 can (6 oz) chunk white tuna, drained
1 c frozen peas, thawed
1/2 c mayonnaise
1/2 c sour cream
4 bacon slices, cooked and crumbled
1/4 c green onion, sliced
1/4 tsp pepper

Boil potatoes until tender. Combine all remaining ingredients; mix well. Serve warm or chilled.

Feta Cheese Potato Salad

12 small potatoes, halved
1/2 c feta cheese
juice of 2 lemons
2 cloves garlic
1/3 c extra-virgin olive oil
1/2 tsp salt
black pepper, freshly ground
leaves from 2 sprigs fresh oregano
1 green onion
1/2 c imported black olives, pitted and slivered

Boil potatoes until soft.

Place all remaining ingredients except olives in the bowl of a food processor fitted with a steel blade. Process until creamy smooth. Reserve.

When potatoes are done, drain well and place in a deep bowl. Add olives.

Pour reserved feta sauce over potatoes and olives. Toss gently but thoroughly.

Serve immediately.

Eggplant Rollatini

2 European eggplants, ends trimmed and
sliced into quarter-inch slices
1/3 c extra virgin olive oil
salt and pepper to taste
1/4 c golden raisins
2 tbsp balsamic vinegar
1 1/2 lb fresh and tender spinach leaves
1/2 tsp salt
1/4 c pitted, imported and dry-cured
black olives, coarsely chopped
1/2 c smoked mozzarella, shredded

Sauce

6 ripe plum tomatoes, chopped into
quarter-inch pieces
1 large clove garlic, minced
1/4 c fresh mint leaves, chopped
3 to 4 tbsp extra-virgin olive oil

Preheat grill or broiler. Rub both sides of
eggplant slices with oil and lightly sprinkle with
salt and pepper. Place on grill and cook for
approximately 6 minutes. Turn and cook an
additional 3 to 4 minutes. Eggplant should be
soft and pliable but not falling apart.

Broiler method: Place eggplant on foil-lined
cookie sheet and set under broiler, watching
carefully to prevent burning. When tops soften
and begin to brown, turn and cook other side.
Cool eggplant strips.

Meanwhile, rehydrate raisins by soaking in
balsamic vinegar and 2 tablespoons hot water.
Rinse spinach; do not dry. Place in a deep pot
with 1/2 teaspoon salt; cover. Cook over
medium heat until spinach wilts, approximately

10 minutes; drain.

Heat heavy-bottomed sauté pan over medium
heat for 20 to 30 seconds; add remaining 1/3
cup oil.

When oil begins to ripple, add wilted spinach
and quickly shake pan for about 2 minutes,
tossing spinach to mix. Add raisins and liquid to
sauté pan; stir well to mix with spinach.
Remove from heat.

When mixture has cooled, add olives and
mozzarella; season with salt and pepper to taste.
Set aside.

Drain excess water by placing mixture in a
colander with a bowl underneath and
refrigerating overnight.

No more than 1 hour before packing picnic, fill
eggplant by placing a small amount of spinach
mixture in center of each strip and bringing both
ends of eggplant over stuffing.

Place seam-side down in a container and
drizzle with a fruity olive oil; secure with a
tight-fitting lid.

Sauce

Combine chopped tomatoes, garlic, mint, and
olive oil; stir well. Refrigerate overnight to
allow flavors to blend.

Red Potato Salad

8 small red potatoes, quartered
1/4 small red onion, diced
3 tbsp capers, drained
1 red bell pepper, roasted, peeled, and chopped
4 tbsp fresh Italian parsley, chopped
2 tbsp fresh basil leaves, chopped
2 tbsp coarse-grained Dijon mustard
1 tsp sugar
1 tbsp champagne vinegar
2 tbsp lemon juice
zest of one lemon
3/4 tsp salt
black pepper, freshly ground
1/4 c plus 2 tbsp extra-virgin olive oil

Place potatoes in a pan to boil. Meanwhile place red onion, capers, bell pepper, and parsley in a medium-sized bowl.

Blend all remaining ingredients except olive oil in the bowl of a food processor. While machine is running, slowly add oil until all is incorporated. Stop machine.

When potatoes are tender, drain, then place in bowl with onion mixture. Pour dressing over potatoes and toss gently until completely mixed. Refrigerate.

Garlic-Roasted New Potatoes

12 to 16 new potatoes, scrubbed clean
1 1/2 tbsp extra-virgin olive oil
4 cloves garlic, minced
1/2 tsp salt
fresh black pepper
4 tbsp extra-virgin olive oil
1 small bunch fresh basil, leaves only

Preheat oven to 400°F.

Peel off a ring of red skin from the middle of each potato; set peels aside. Toss potatoes with 1 1/2 tablespoons olive oil; place in a shallow baking pan.

Roast for 30 to 40 minutes, moving them a couple of times during baking so that they brown evenly.

Meanwhile, place remaining ingredients and potato peel rings in the bowl of a food processor fitted with a steel blade. Process until all are minced.

When potatoes are done, remove from oven and toss with processed ingredients. Allow to cool; store in refrigerator.

Texas Caviar

1 can black-eyed peas, drained
1 can white hominy, drained and chopped
2 or 3 green onions, chopped
1/2 c onion, chopped
1 green bell pepper, chopped
2 medium tomatoes, chopped
2 cloves garlic, minced
1/3 c parsley, chopped
1 c picante sauce
1 c shoepeg corn
salt and pepper

Mix all ingredients, cover, and allow to sit for a day. Season with salt and pepper to taste. Serve with small round corn chips.

Mixed Vegetable Grill with Feta

2 c zucchini, sliced in half-inch slices
1 pkg (4 oz) feta cheese, crumbled
1 c green pepper, cut into 1/2-inch strips
1 c tomato wedges
1/2 c onion, cut into 1/4-inch rings
1 tbsp fresh oregano, chopped and crushed
1 tbsp olive oil

Mix all ingredients. Wrap mixture in double thickness of aluminum foil. Grill 10 minutes over medium-hot coals. Turn packet over and grill 8 minutes more or until vegetables are tender. Makes 6 servings.

Boston Baked Beans

1 lb pea or navy beans
water
2 tsp dry mustard
1/4 tsp pepper
1 tsp salt
3 onions, quartered
1/4 c brown sugar
1/4 c molasses
2 tbsp sweet pickle juice
1/8 tsp ground cinnamon
1/8 tsp ground cloves
1/4 lb salt pork, cubed

Remove debris from and wash beans. Cover with 3 cups of water and soak for 8 hours or overnight. Drain beans and wash. Add 2 cups water, mustard, pepper and next 5 ingredients. Boil, covered, about 1 hour or until skins start to wrinkle. If necessary, add additional water to prevent beans from burning. Preheat oven to 250°F. Place pork, then beans, including liquid, in beanpot. Sprinkle with pepper and bake 6-8 hours or until tender. When beans are two-thirds baked, add about 3/4 cup water or just enough to cover. Uncover during last half hour of baking.

Papaya-Salmon Pasta Salad

1 lb pasta
6 tbsp vegetable oil
fresh ground black pepper to taste
1 lb skinless and boneless, fresh or frozen
    salmon fillets, cooked and chopped,
    or 2 cans (7 1/2 oz ea) salmon, drained
    and flaked
1 papaya, peeled, seeded or 15 oz
    canned papaya in light syrup, drained
    and chopped
1 c cherry tomatoes
1 bunch scallions, sliced fine
1 yellow bell pepper, seeded, ribs removed,
    and chopped
1 medium cucumber, quartered lengthwise
    and sliced
1 small jalapeño, seeded, ribs removed,
    and minced fine
2 tbsp fresh cilantro, chopped or 2 tsp
    dried cilantro
3 tbsp rice wine vinegar
3 tbsp white wine vinegar
3 drops hot sauce

Prepare pasta according to package directions; drain and transfer to a medium bowl. While pasta is still warm, mix in vegetable oil. Season with black pepper. Set pasta aside to cool.

In a medium mixing bowl, add salmon, papaya, tomatoes, scallions, yellow pepper, and cucumber. Toss together with pasta.

In a small bowl, combine jalapeño, cilantro, both vinegars, and hot sauce. Toss pasta with dressing and refrigerate.

Chill well before serving.

Campfire Cooking

Zest:
To remove the outmost skin of citrus fruit with a knife, peeler, or zester. Be careful not to remove the pith (the white layer between the zest and the flesh), which is very bitter.

Drizzle:
To pour a liquid, such as butter or melted chocolate, over food in a thin stream.

Apple Delights

12 large apples
4 tbsp sugar
3/4 c biscuit mix
raisins
3 tbsp cinnamon

For each Apple Delight, core and chop one apple in fairly large pieces. Mix one teaspoon sugar, a few raisins and cinnamon to taste with one tablespoon biscuit mix. Stir into chopped apple. Wrap in a piece of greased aluminum foil, leaving sufficient space for steam. Cook in embers 30 to 45 minutes. (Juice of apple moistens dough sufficiently.)

Baked Apples

12 large, ripe apples
1 c nuts
1 c coconut, shredded
12 dates
1 c brown sugar
12 marshmallows

Remove cores from apples, being sure not to cut through skin at one end. Fill hole with nuts, dates, and coconut. Sprinkle well with brown sugar. Wrap with foil and place in embers. When tender, toast a marshmallow and place on apple. Bakes in about 20 minutes.

Campfire Apple Cobbler

4 c apples, sliced
1 1/3 c sugar
1 tsp. cinnamon
2 c biscuit mix (or pie crust mix)

Mix sugar and cinnamon with sliced apples and cook in saucepan until apples are tender. (Canned apple slices may be used instead.)

Spread cooked apples in 2 shallow, 8-inch pie pans. Prepare dough from biscuit or pie crust mix according to package directions.

Roll prepared dough with a round jar or small log between two pieces of waxed paper. Place a circle of dough on pie filling.

Set pie pan on a sheet of foil, leaving half of foil exposed. Fold exposed portion on three edges up and over the pie pan to form a small oven.

Set either on the ground or on rocks before a hot blazing fire. The portion of the pie under the foil will brown first from reflected heat.

Turn pie within the foil oven to brown evenly. Bake 15 to 20 minutes.

Potatonions

12 medium potatoes
12 medium onions, sliced in rounds
salt and pepper to taste
1/4 c butter or margarine

For each Potatonion, cut potato into 4 crosswise slices. Spread butter on both sides of each slice.

Place half an onion (sliced in rounds) between potato slices; season with salt and pepper. Secure slices with toothpicks or skewers and wrap tightly in foil.

Bake in embers for 30 to 40 minutes.

Maria's Burger Dinner

12 potatoes, cut into small pieces
12 carrots, cut into sticks
1 large onion, diced
3 lb ground beef
salt and pepper to taste

For each burger, pat 1/4 pound ground beef into a 3/4-inch thick patty.

Place patty, 1 cut-up potato, 1 cut-up carrot, and some onion side-by-side on a piece of aluminum foil. Season to taste.

Wrap up and put foil packet in embers. Cook 20 minutes.

Try this with other food combinations such as ham, pineapple, and sweet potatoes (with a touch of brown sugar); chicken, corn, and potatoes; hot dogs and onions; hot dogs with cheese and bacon; or hot dogs with apples and cheese. Or make up your own family favorite!

Fireside Beef Stew

3 lb beef, cut into 1-inch chunks
12 bacon slices, cut into pieces
12 tomatoes, quartered
6 onions, sliced

Place 1/4 pound of beef, 1 slice bacon, 1 quartered tomato, and half a sliced onion in aluminum foil packet. Cook in embers 30 to 40 minutes. Makes 12 servings.

Pigs in a Blanket

4 c flour
2 tbsp baking powder
1 tsp salt
3 tbsp sugar
6 tbsp shortening
water or milk for desired consistency
24 link-style pork sausages, seared
   in a hot skillet

Mix dough as for biscuits. Pinch off small pieces of dough and flatten into strips or elongated patties. Wrap each seared sausage link in a strip of dough. Knead sides of dough together so that sausage is completely covered. Wrap in foil and cook for 15 minutes.

Shrimp Barbecue

4 lb large green shrimp, peeled and cleaned
1 c butter or margarine
1 large clove garlic, minced
1/2 tsp black pepper
1 tsp. salt
1 c parsley, minced

Cream butter; add remaining ingredients to butter and mix well.

Cut 6 nine-inch strips of heavy-duty aluminum foil. Then cut each strip in half. Divide shrimp equally on each piece of foil, topping with butter mixture; twist and seal tightly. Place shrimp packets on embers. Cook 5 minutes. Makes 12 servings.

Stuffed Trout

12 medium trout
3 medium onions, finely chopped
1/4 lb butter or margarine

Clean fish thoroughly; season insides with salt and pepper. Fill each fish about 3/4 full with onion; place a pat of butter on top of onion.

Wrap each fish separately in aluminum foil. Bury in hot embers and bake 20 to 25 minutes.

Barbecue Chicken Wrap Sandwiches

1 lb boneless and skinless chicken breasts
1 medium onion, sliced
2 medium green peppers, quartered
1 c barbecue sauce
8 flour tortillas (6-inch)

Place chicken and vegetables on greased grill over medium-hot coals.

Grill chicken 5-6 minutes on each side or until cooked through and vegetables 4-5 minutes on each side, brushing each frequently with sauce.

Slice chicken and vegetables into thin strips. Divide strips among tortillas.

Roll up tortillas. Serve with additional sauce, if desired.

Grill Potato and Onion Packages

2/3 c olive oil
1 tbsp Dijon mustard
2 tbsp fresh thyme, chopped or 1 tbsp dried thyme
1 tsp salt
1 tsp ground black pepper
2 lb (about 4 large) white-skinned potatoes, peeled and sliced into 1/4-inch thick slices
2 large red onions, halved and sliced into 1/2-inch thick slices
cooking spray
salt and pepper to taste
sprigs of fresh thyme (optional)

Combine oil, mustard, thyme, salt, and pepper in large bowl. Whisk to blend well. (Can be prepared up to 6 hours before cooking. Cover and let stand at room temperature.)

Prepare barbecue for medium-high heat. Add potatoes and onions to mustard oil; toss to coat. Set six 18x9-inch sheets of heavy-duty aluminum foil on work surface. Spray foil with cooking spray. Divide vegetables among foil sheets, placing in center of left half of each sheet. Sprinkle with salt and pepper. Fold right half of foil over vegetables. Fold edges of packages together to seal tightly.

Place packages on grill. Grill until potatoes are tender and golden brown, turning occasionally, about 25 minutes. Remove packages from grill. Slit top of foil and fold back.

Perfect for Picnics

Scald:

To bring to a temperature just below boiling so that
tiny bubbles form at the edges of a pan.

Kielbasa:

A smoked sausage of coarsely chopped beef and pork,
flavored with spices. Also called *Polish Sausage*.

Figs and Sweet Mascarpone Cheese

6 fresh black mission figs
2 c mascarpone cheese
3 tbsp confectioners' sugar
zest of half an orange
sprigs of fresh mint

Place mascarpone cheese, confectioners' sugar, and orange zest in the bowl of a food processor. Pulse until ingredients are just combined. Refrigerate until ready to use.

To serve, halve figs, placing three pieces on each plate with a dollop of cheese mixture. Garnish each plate with a fresh mint sprig.

Muffuletta Sandwich with Olive Salad

1 10-inch loaf Muffuletta bread
   (or French bread)
2 oz Genoa salami, thinly sliced
2 oz Italian ham, thinly sliced
2 oz Provolone cheese, thinly sliced
1 cup Olive Salad (recipe follows)

Cut bread in half crosswise. Pile several layers of salami and ham on bottom layer. Add layers of cheese. Top with Olive Salad and top of loaf. Press down lightly and cut into quarters. Makes 1 to 4 servings.

Olive Salad

1 jar (32 oz) broken green olives (unstuffed)
6 cloves garlic, minced
2 jars (3 1/4 oz each) marinated cocktail
   onions, drained (approximately 1 c)
4 celery stalks, halved lengthwise
   and thinly sliced

1 jar (4 oz) pimentos, chopped and drained
2 tbsp capers, chopped and drained
1 tbsp dried leaf oregano or 3 tbsp
   fresh oregano, chopped
1 tsp finely ground black pepper
3 tbsp red-wine vinegar
1/3 c olive oil

Drain olives; reserve 3 tablespoons brine. In medium bowl, combine olives, garlic, onions, celery, pimentos, and capers. In small bowl, whisk reserved brine, oregano, pepper, and vinegar until combined. Add olive oil in a slow, steady stream, whisking constantly. Pour brine mixture over vegetables; toss. Spoon into a jar with a tight-fitting lid. Refrigerate until served or up to 3 weeks.

Serve at room temperature. Makes about 5 cups.

Picnic Chicken Salad Sandwiches

1 can (10 3/4 oz) cream of celery soup
2 tbsp mayonnaise
1/4 tsp pepper
2 c chicken, cooked and chopped
2 stalks celery, sliced (about 1 c)
1 small onion, finely chopped (about 1/4 c)
6 round sandwich rolls, split
lettuce leaves
tomato slices

In medium bowl, mix soup, mayonnaise, and pepper. Stir in chicken, celery, and onion. Refrigerate at least 4 hours.

Divide chicken mixture among 6 roll halves. Top with lettuce, tomato, and remaining roll halves. Makes 6 sandwiches.

Picnic Macaroni Salad

2 c macaroni, cooked
2 eggs, hard-boiled and chopped
1 tbsp green onion, minced
1/4 c sweet pickle, minced (or 2 tbsp relish)
1/4 c celery, finely diced
1 tbsp capers
1 c frozen green peas, cooked
2 tbsp pimento, chopped

Dressing
1/2 c mayonnaise
2 tbsp pickle juice (omit if using relish)
1 tsp prepared mustard
1/4 tsp pepper
1 tsp salt
2 tbsp sour cream
2 tbsp parsley, chopped

Place macaroni in large bowl. Add egg, onion, pickle, celery, capers, peas, and pimentos. Combine dressing ingredients and add to macaroni mixture. Toss lightly with 2 forks to combine. Chill before serving.

Fussily Michel

1 can (15 oz) stewed tomatoes
1/2 c sun-dried tomatoes, julienned
1/4 lb. mushrooms, julienned
1/4 c (packed) fresh basil leaves
1 to 2 cloves garlic, pressed
1 to 2 tbsp olive oil
salt and pepper to taste
1 pkg (10 oz) fussily, cooked and drained

Heat olive oil in a saucepan and briefly sauté vegetables (about 3 minutes). Drain canned tomatoes and purée in blender until almost smooth.

Add basil leaves to vegetables and sauté, stirring constantly, for about 30 seconds.

Add tomato purée. Stir in garlic and black pepper. Cook for 5 minutes. Add salt to taste. Toss over cooked fussily.

Fussily al Carbone

1 lb. collards, coarsely chopped
   and coarse stems discarded
1/4 lb. bacon slices, cut into 1/2-inch pieces
4 large cloves garlic, finely chopped
1 large onion, thinly sliced
1/4 tsp dried hot red pepper flakes
1/3 c olive oil
3/4 lb. fussily
1 tbsp red-wine vinegar
Parmesan cheese, freshly grated
salt and pepper to taste

In a pot of boiling water, boil collards for 10 minutes. Drain in a colander set over a large bowl, and return cooking liquid to pot. Cook bacon over moderate heat in a large skillet, stirring constantly, until it is just browned. Transfer bacon with a slotted spoon to a small bowl. Pour off fat from skillet and cook garlic, onion, and hot red pepper flakes in half of oil over moderately low heat, stirring constantly, until onion is softened and garlic is golden brown.

Bring cooking liquid to a boil and cook fussily until it is *al dente*; drain well. To skillet, add collards, bacon, fussily, remaining oil, and vinegar. Toss well. Season fussily with salt and pepper. Divide among 4 bowls and sprinkle each serving with Parmesan cheese.

Mama's Burger Buns

3 c all-purpose flour (plus additional
  flour for kneading)
2 c whole-wheat flour
1/3 c toasted wheat germ
2 pkg active dry yeast
2 tsp salt
2 c milk
1/4 c sugar
1/4 c solid vegetable shortening

Place 1 1/2 cups all-purpose flour, 1 1/2 cups whole-wheat flour, toasted wheat germ, yeast, and salt in a large bowl. Briefly mix together with an electric mixer. (A heavy-duty one, with a paddle attachment, is preferred.)

Melt shortening in a saucepan over low heat. Add milk and sugar; heat until sugar is dissolved and mixture is very warm, but no hotter than 120° or 130°F. With mixer at low speed, slowly pour milk mixture into flour mixture until blended.

Increase to medium speed and beat mixture for about 2 minutes. Add 1/2 cup white flour and 1/2 cup whole-wheat flour and beat 2 minutes more. Add 1 cup all-purpose flour and beat until dough comes away from sides of bowl.

On a lightly floured surface, knead dough about 8 minutes or until smooth and elastic. (Use very little additional flour.) Place in bowl, cover with plastic wrap, and set aside to rise in a warm place until double in volume, about 1 or 1 1/2 hours.

Gently punch dough down and divide into 4 equal portions. Divide each portion into fourths and allow dough to rest just 5 minutes. Form the small portions into balls and with fingertips fold edges under to form even circles. Place about 2 inches apart on lightly greased baking sheets; with fingertips flatten each bun to a 3-inch circle. (To keep the sides of the buns soft, place circles closer together. Then as buns rise sides will touch.)

Cover with a towel and set aside to rise until doubled, about 1 hour.

Adjust rack in lower third of oven. Preheat oven to 350°F at least 20 minutes before baking. Bake for 15 to 20 minutes or until buns are golden and sound hollow when tapped lightly.

Cool completely on wire rack before slicing. (Or cool and freeze, well-wrapped, for up to 1 week.) Makes 16.

To form hot dog buns: Divide dough in half. On a lightly floured surface, pat or roll out each portion to a rectangle about 14x5 inches. Cut about eight 5x2-inch strips from each rectangle. Roll each portion between palms of hands into 6-inch long buns.

Place buns about two inches apart on lightly greased baking sheets. Cover loosely with a cloth towel and set aside in a warm place until doubled, about 1 hour. Bake as directed for hamburger buns. Makes 16.

Sesame Seed Buns

After shaping buns, lightly brush tops with 1 egg white which has been lightly beaten with 1 teaspoon water. Sprinkle sesame seeds over glaze. Cover lightly with a towel and allow buns to rise before baking.

Picnic Pita

1 1/2 c cucumbers, chopped
1 1/2 c tomatoes, chopped
1/2 c Thousand Island dressing
6 pita breads, cut in half
6 slices cheese, halved
1 pkg (6-oz) sliced ham
1 pkg (6-oz) sliced turkey

Mix cucumbers, tomatoes, and dressing. Spoon 2 tablespoons cucumber mixture into each pita half. Fill with remaining ingredients. Makes 6 sandwiches.

Mushroom and Walnut Crostini

This recipe lends itself well to a picnic because it can be made up to 2 days ahead of time and can be packed easily.

3 to 4 tbsp extra-virgin olive oil
3 c mushrooms, cleaned and coarsely chopped
1 clove garlic, minced
2 green onions, thinly sliced
1 pkg (8 oz) low-fat cream cheese
2 tbsp soy sauce
2 tbsp non-fat sour cream
2 tbsp sherry
1/2 c walnuts, toasted and finely chopped
1/4 c Italian parsley, chopped

Heat a heavy-bottomed sauté pan over medium heat for approximately 20 to 30 seconds. Add 2 tablespoons olive oil and tip pan to coat bottom. Quickly add garlic and green onions and sauté for 1 to 2 minutes; remove from heat. Add remaining oil and mushrooms, shaking pan regularly. Cook for 8-10 minutes or until mushrooms release their juices. Remove from heat and cool.

Meanwhile, place green onions, garlic, and all remaining ingredients except walnuts and parsley in the bowl of a food processor. Mix until smooth and creamy. Stir into cooled mushrooms, adding walnuts and parsley while mixing ingredients together.

Crostini

1 small baguette
small amount of extra-virgin olive oil

Preheat oven to 375°F. Slice bread into quarter-inch thickness. Lightly brush one side with olive oil; place on a cookie sheet with oiled side up. Bake for 10 minutes, then turn to brown other side. Remove. Cool completely before storing. Will make enough for this picnic plus leftovers.

Picnic Chicken

1/2 c fresh lemon juice
6 garlic cloves
1 bay leaf
1/2 tsp dried thyme
1/2 tsp dried marjoram
1/2 tsp dried summer savory
4 1/2 to 5 lb roasting chicken
salt and pepper

Combine first 6 ingredients in blender and blend until garlic and bay leaf are finely chopped. Transfer mixture to bowl. Add chicken to bowl and turn to coat. Marinate chicken in bowl in refrigerator, breast side down, overnight.

Preheat oven to 375°F. Place rack in roasting pan. Remove chicken from marinade, reserving marinade. Place chicken on prepared rack and season with salt and pepper. Roast in oven until chicken is cooked through, basting occasionally with reserved marinade, about 1 hour and 20 minutes.

Caribbean Picnic Pie

3/4 c whole wheat flour
1/2 c unbleached white flour
1 tsp sugar
1/2 tsp salt
1/2 tsp dried thyme
zest and juice of 1 lime
1/4 c cold water
3 tbsp olive oil
1 medium red potato, diced
1 small yam, peeled and diced
1 small yellow onion, sliced
1/4 c red bell pepper, diced
3 cloves garlic, minced
1/2 tsp thyme
1/2 tsp ground ginger
1/2 tsp black pepper
1/2 tsp cinnamon
1/4 tsp ground cayenne pepper
1/4 tsp nutmeg
1/4 tsp cloves
1/4 tsp allspice
1 c spinach, chopped and packed
1 tbsp sun-dried tomato, minced
2 tbsp soy sauce
2 tbsp red wine vinegar
1 tsp Dijon mustard

In a medium mixing bowl, whisk together flours, sugar, salt, and dried thyme. Make a well in center and add lime zest, juice, water, and 2 tablespoons oil. Stir with a spoon, then press dough together forming a ball.

Transfer ball from hand to hand, pressing it until it holds together well. Gently knead a few times, flatten ball into a disk, wrap in plastic and set aside.

In a large skillet over medium heat, sauté potato, yam, onion, carrot, bell pepper, garlic, and spices in 1 tablespoon oil, stirring frequently, for 10 minutes or until slightly soft. Stir in spinach and tomato.

In a small bowl, whisk together soy sauce, vinegar, and mustard and add to skillet.

Stir to deglaze pan and coat vegetables with juices. Remove from heat and set aside.

Preheat oven to 350°F and spray a pie pan with cooking spray. Place dough between layers of plastic wrap or waxed paper and roll out into a 13-inch circle; transfer to prepared pan.

Mound filling in center, leaving a border of dough about 6 inches wide all around.

Gather edges of dough up and over filling, toward center, pleating and pressing while gathering, to form a deep, flattened, pouch-like pie about 7 inches in diameter with an opening on top about 3 inches across.

Bake for 1 hour and 15 minutes or until potatoes are tender and crust is browned.

Desserts

Baste:
To brush or spoon food as it cooks with melted fat
or the cooking juices from the dish.

Blanch:
To immerse briefly in boiling water.

Chocolate Chip Cookie Dough Ice Cream

2 c milk
1 3/4 c sugar
1/2 tsp salt
2 c half-and-half
1 tbsp vanilla extract
4 c whipping cream
1 large pkg chocolate chip cookie dough

Remove cookie dough from refrigerator and allow to soften until needed.

Scald milk until bubbles form around edge; remove from heat. Add sugar and salt; stir until dissolved. Stir in half-and-half, vanilla, and whipping cream. Cover and refrigerate 30 minutes. Freeze in ice cream freezer per manufacturer's instructions.

When ice cream reaches the chilled, soft ice cream stage, add the chocolate chip cookie dough. Use hands to break dough and drop it in small clusters into soft ice cream. Mix to ensure that cookie dough is evenly distributed throughout ice cream. Process ice cream in freezer for several hours until hardened.

Gingersnap Ice Cream

1/2 c raisins, chopped
2 tbsp rum (optional)
4 large eggs, lightly beaten
2 c milk
1 c sugar
3 c whipping cream
2 tbsp molasses
1 tbsp vanilla extract
1 c gingersnaps (12 to 15 cookies), crumbled

Combine raisins and rum, if desired; set aside.

Combine eggs, milk, and sugar in a heavy saucepan; cook, stirring constantly, until mixture thickens and coats a spoon. Remove from heat; cool. Cover and chill.

Stir in raisin mixture, whipping cream, molasses, and vanilla; gently stir in gingersnaps. Pour into freezer container of a one-gallon hand-turned or electric freezer. Freeze according to manufacturer's instructions.

Basic Homemade Ice Cream

1 1/2 qt milk
2 c sugar
1 container (8 oz) frozen whipped topping, thawed
1 can (12 oz) evaporated milk
1 pkg (5.1 oz) vanilla instant pudding mix

Combine all ingredients, stirring well. Pour mixture into freezer container of a one-gallon hand-turned or electric freezer. Freeze according to manufacturer's instructions.

Variations: This ice cream can be made in different flavors by using a different flavor pudding mix or by adding nuts.

Add fruit by combining 1 1/2 cups puréed fresh fruit and 1/4 cup sugar, stirring into ice cream mixture and freezing as directed.

Peach Frozen Yogurt

2 c low-fat vanilla yogurt
1/4 c honey
1/4 c maple syrup
2 large peaches, peeled and quartered

Process all ingredients in a blender or food processor until smooth, stopping once to scrape mixture from sides. Pour mixture into freezer container of a one-gallon hand-turned or electric freezer. Freeze according to manufacturer's instructions.

(Note: It is recommended that ripe, fragrant peaches with no blemishes be used.)

Easy Homemade Chocolate Ice Cream

2 c (1 pt) cold whipping cream
1 c chocolate syrup, chilled
1 tsp vanilla extract

In large bowl, beat whipping cream until stiff. Gently fold in syrup and vanilla. Spoon into 8-inch square pan or 9x5x2-inch loaf pan. Cover; freeze about 1 hour or until partially frozen; stir to break up ice crystals. Continue freezing several hours or until firm.

Cookies and Cream: Break chocolate sandwich creme-filled cookies (about 8) into small pieces to equal 1 cup. Fold into chocolate mixture before freezing.

Cherry Chocolate Cream: Cut 1-1/2 cups pitted ripe sweet cherries into quarters. In small saucepan, combine cherries with 1/4 cup sugar; heat to boiling, stirring constantly. Remove from heat; cool completely. Drain; fold into chocolate mixture before freezing.

Melt-In-Your-Mouth Blueberry Cake

2 eggs, separated
1 c sugar, divided
1/2 c butter, softened
1/4 tsp salt
1 tsp vanilla
1 1/2 c flour, sifted
1 tbsp flour for coating berries
1 tsp baking powder
1/3 c milk
1 1/2 c fresh blueberries
cinnamon sugar for topping

Preheat oven to 350°F. Beat egg whites until stiff. Beat in 1/4 cup of sugar.

In another bowl, cream butter; gradually add salt, vanilla, and remaining sugar. Add egg yolks and beat until creamy.

Sift flour with baking powder. Alternate adding flour, baking powder and milk to creamed mixture. Fold in beaten egg whites.

Coat blueberries with 1 tablespoon of flour; fold into mixture. Turn into 8x8-inch pan.

Sprinkle with cinnamon sugar and bake for 50 minutes. Cool on rack.

Wrap any leftovers and store in refrigerator. May be frozen.

Old-Fashioned Apple Pie with Vanilla-Coconut Ice Cream and Butterscotch Drizzle

Pastry crust

2 1/4 c all-purpose flour
2/3 c plus 2 tbsp vegetable shortening
pinch of salt
5 to 6 tbsp ice water

Preheat oven to 425°F. In a mixing bowl, blend flour, shortening, and salt with a pastry cutter until mixture resembles coarse meal. Blend in enough water to make mixture just cling together to form a ball. Divide pastry in half and shape each half into a flat disk. Roll first disk into an 11-inch circle on a lightly-floured board. Transfer to a 9-inch pie pan and trim over-hanging pastry edges half an inch from rim of pan.

Pie filling

7 c McIntosh apples, peeled, cored,
  and thinly sliced
1 c granulated sugar
1/2 tsp ground cinnamon
1/2 tsp ground nutmeg
2 tbsp all-purpose flour
1 tbsp unsalted butter

Combine apples, sugar, cinnamon, nutmeg, and flour in a large mixing bowl and toss well to coat apples evenly. Mound filling into pie shell. Dot top with butter cut into small bits.

Roll out remaining disk of pastry into an 11-inch circle. Place over apples, then trim and crimp pastry edges together decoratively.

Brush milk lightly and evenly over top crust and then sprinkle with sugar. Using a sharp paring knife, cut 4 or 5 slits into top crust to allow steam to escape during baking. Bake 40 to 45 minutes until crust is golden brown.

Vanilla-Coconut Ice Cream

1 pt vanilla ice cream, softened
1/3 c cream of coconut
1 1/2 c flaked coconut, lightly toasted

Combine softened vanilla ice cream with cream of coconut and toasted coconut in a food processor fitted with a steel blade. Process until mixture is smooth and well combined. Transfer mixture into a freezer container. Freeze until firm.

Butterscotch Drizzle

6 tbsp unsalted butter
1 c packed dark brown sugar
1/3 c dark corn syrup
1/2 c heavy cream
1 tsp vanilla extract

Melt 4 tablespoons butter in a saucepan over medium heat. Add brown sugar, corn syrup, cream, and vanilla; stir until smooth. Bring mixture to a full boil; let boil undisturbed for 3 minutes. Remove from heat and add remaining 2 tablespoons butter, stirring until melted. Sauce may be served warm or at room temperature; leftover sauce will keep indefinitely if refrigerated and stored in a jar.

Serve pie warm or at room temperature. Cut it into wedges and top each serving with a scoop of Vanilla-Coconut Ice Cream. Drizzle butterscotch sauce in back and forth motions over both pie and ice cream. Serve at once.

Shortcake Ring with Strawberries

2 c all-purpose flour
3 tbsp sugar
3 tsp fresh baking powder
1/2 tsp baking soda
1/2 tsp salt
6 tbsp unsalted butter, chilled
2 tbsp solid all-vegetable shortening, chilled
2/3 to 3/4 c buttermilk

Adjust rack in lower third of the oven and preheat to 450°F. Generously grease a 9-inch ring mold (or an 8-inch cake pan).

Sift dry ingredients into a large bowl. Cut butter into half-inch slices. With a pastry blender, cut butter into dry ingredients until butter pieces are the size of lima beans.

Cut in the shortening until mixture looks like coarse meal.

Slowly stir in buttermilk with a fork until mixture forms a dough that leaves the sides of the bowl. (Do not overmix.)

Gently knead dough on a lightly floured board about five to six times until dough holds together (it should be soft). Be careful not to add too much additional flour during kneading.

With a lightly floured hand, pat dough lightly (just using fingertips) to one-inch thickness and pat into ring mold.

Bake about 18 to 20 minutes or until golden. Remove to rack to cool 5 minutes, then invert from pan onto another wire rack, bottom side up. Cool before adding filling.

Filling
2 pt fresh strawberries
2 tbsp sugar
1/2 pt heavy cream, whipped
2 tbsp powdered sugar

Slice berries in half, sprinkle with two tablespoons sugar and allow to sit at least 30 minutes, stirring occasionally.

Remove half of strawberries to another bowl and coarsely mash with a pastry blender or fork. Let both bowls of strawberries sit at least an additional 30 minutes.

When cool, set shortcake ring on a serving plate. Carefully split ring into two layers with a serrated knife. With the aid of another pan or baking sheet, lift top shortcake portion and set it nearby. (Baking sheet bottom supports shortcake ring and prevents it from breaking.)

Spoon mashed berries and their juice over biscuit bottom, spread lightly whipped cream on top of berries, then arrange berry halves on top of cream.

Using baking sheet, set shortcake ring half on top. Sprinkle powdered sugar lightly over top. Serve immediately.

Strawberry Rhubarb Crisp

6 strawberries, sliced
4 c rhubarb, cut into one-inch pieces
3/4 c white sugar
1 egg, lightly beaten
1 tsp vanilla extract
3/4 c flour
3/4 c brown sugar
3/4 stick butter, melted

Preheat oven to 350°F.

Place strawberries and rhubarb in a bowl and toss with white sugar, egg, and vanilla. Transfer mixture to a large baking dish. Mix flour, brown sugar, and melted butter together in a bowl until mixture crumbles and resembles peas. Sprinkle mixture over fruit in baking dish. Bake 45 to 60 minutes or until mixture is bubbling and top is browned and crisp. Remove from oven and allow to cool. Cover with aluminum foil and keep at room temperature. This is best eaten the same day when topping is the most crunchy.

Apple Pie Cake

1/2 c butter
3/4 c sugar
1 egg, slightly beaten
1 c flour
1 tsp baking powder
1 tsp ground cinnamon
1/2 tsp salt
1/2 tsp ground nutmeg
1/2 tsp ground cloves
1/8 tsp vanilla
2 c apples, peeled and chopped
1/2 c pecans, chopped

Preheat oven to 350° F. Thoroughly grease a 9-inch pie pan. Melt butter, remove from heat, and blend with sugar and egg. Mix in flour, baking powder, cinnamon, salt, nutmeg, cloves, vanilla, apples, and pecans. Spread into pan. Bake for 40-45 minutes. Serve warm with ice cream.

Lemon Afternoon Delight

8 oz cream cheese, softened
1/2 c mayonnaise
1/2 c sugar
3 eggs
1 tsp vanilla
2 tsp lemon rind, grated
1 tbsp lemon juice (optional)
1 graham cracker crust

In large bowl with mixer at medium speed, beat cream cheese and mayonnaise until smooth; gradually beat in sugar. One at a time, beat in eggs; then beat in lemon rind, lemon juice, and vanilla. Pour into pie crust; place on cookie sheet. Bake at 350° F for 30-45 minutes or until set. Chill 4 hours.

Chess Pie

1 unbaked 9-inch pie crust
1/2 c butter, melted
1 1/2 c sugar
3 eggs
1 tsp vanilla
pinch salt
3/4 tbsp vinegar

Prepare unbaked pie shell. Mix butter and sugar and simmer slowly, stirring constantly, for 5 minutes. Remove from heat and let cool slightly, stirring constantly. Add eggs, one at a time, beating well. Add vanilla, salt, and vinegar; mix well. Pour filling into pie shell and bake at 400° F for 15 minutes; reduce heat to 350° F and bake for 20-30 minutes. Shake pie gently. Pie is done when center quivers slightly. Do not try to double recipe. Pie keeps well in refrigerator overnight. Can freeze and reheat.

Sweet Heaven Delight

2 sticks butter
2 c flour
1 c pecans, chopped
1/2 c powdered sugar
2 pkg. (8 oz ea) cream cheese
2 c whipped topping
2 c powdered sugar
2 c cooked sweet potato purée
whipped topping (for garnish)
pecans, chopped (for garnish)

Melt butter; add flour, 1 cup nuts, and 1/2 cup powdered sugar. Press into 9x13-inch baking pan. Bake 15 minutes at 375° F or until lightly browned.

Make filling: Combine cream cheese, 2 cups whipped topping, 2 cups powdered sugar, and sweet potato purée; mix well and spread over cooled first layer. Top with a layer of whipped topping; sprinkle with chopped pecans.

Chocolate Praline Cheesecake

Crust
1 1/3 c graham cracker crumbs
5 tbsp butter, melted
2 tbsp honey

Filling
12 oz semisweet chocolate morsels
1/2 c boiling water
2 tsp instant coffee granules
2 pkg. (8 oz ea) cream cheese, softened
1 c packed brown sugar
4 large eggs
1 c pecans, chopped coarse

Topping
1/2 c packed brown sugar
1/4 c heavy cream
1 tsp butter
pecan halves for garnish

Preheat oven to 350°F.

Crust
Combine crumbs, 5 tablespoons butter, and honey in a 9-inch springform pan. Press mixture evenly onto bottom of pan.

Filling
In top of a double boiler set over simmering (not boiling) water, combine chocolate morsels, water, and coffee. Stir mixture until smooth. Remove top of double boiler from water. Set aside.

In a large mixing bowl, using an electric mixer set on high speed, beat cream cheese and 1 cup brown sugar until smooth and fluffy, about 2 minutes. Add eggs, one at a time, beating after each addition. Add chocolate mixture; beat until smooth. Beat in chopped pecans. Pour over crust; bake cheesecake until center is set, about 1 hour and 25 minutes. Place cheesecake on a wire rack and cool completely. Cover and refrigerate for at least 8 hours.

Topping
In a small saucepan, heat 1/2 cup brown sugar, cream, and 1 teaspoon butter over medium heat, stirring until brown sugar dissolves. Bring mixture to a boil; cook without stirring until syrupy and golden brown, about 1-2 minutes. Remove caramel from heat and let cool for 5 minutes. Pour topping over cheesecake, tilting cake to spread evenly. Garnish, if desired, with pecan halves. Remove side of pan. Serve within 2 hours of topping.

NOTE: Cheesecake (without topping) may be made 3 days in advance. Keep cake tightly covered and refrigerated.

Sweet Potato Log Roll

3 eggs
1 c sugar
3/4 c sweet potatoes, mashed
1 tsp lemon juice
3/4 c all-purpose flour
2 tsp cinnamon
1/4 tsp salt
1 tsp baking powder
1/2 tsp ground cloves
1/4 tsp ground ginger
3/4 c pecans, chopped
powdered sugar
Filling (recipe follows)

Grease and flour bottom and sides of a 15x10x1-inch jelly roll pan; line bottom of pan with waxed paper. Beat eggs at high speed of electric mixer until thick and lemon colored (about 5 minutes); gradually add sugar, beating 5 additional minutes. Continue beating and gradually add sweet potatoes and lemon juice. In a separate bowl, combine flour, cinnamon, salt, baking powder, cloves, and ginger. Stir into sweet potato mixture. Pour batter into prepared pan, spreading evenly. Sprinkle with pecans. Bake at 375°F for 12-15 minutes or until cake turns loose from sides of pan.

Sift powdered sugar in a 15x9-inch rectangle on a woven dish towel. When cake is done, immediately loosen from sides of pan; turn out on sugar. Peel off waxed paper. Starting at narrow edge, roll up cake and towel together; cool on a wire rack, seam side down. When cool, unroll cake and remove towel. Spread cake with filling; reroll. Chill until serving time.

NOTE: Cake may wait up to 24 hours before filling.

Filling

1/4 c butter, softened
4 oz cream cheese, softened
1 c powdered sugar
1/4 tsp butter flavoring
1/2 tsp vanilla flavoring
pinch salt
Combine butter and cream cheese, beating until light and fluffy. Add powdered sugar, flavorings, and salt; beat until smooth.

Gillie Whoopers

3/4 c flour, sifted
1/4 tsp baking powder
1/4 tsp salt
2 tbsp cocoa
3/4 c sugar
1/2 c shortening
2 eggs
1 tsp vanilla
1/2 c walnuts
1 pkg. miniature marshmallows
1/2 c brown sugar
1/4 c water
2 squares baking chocolate
3 tbsp butter
2 tbsp vanilla
1 1/2 c powdered sugar

Combine flour, baking powder, salt, cocoa, and sugar. Blend in shortening, eggs, and 1 teaspoon vanilla. Add walnuts. Spread in greased baking pan and bake at 350°F for 20 minutes. Remove from oven; sprinkle miniature marshmallows over top, keeping them away from sides of pan. Bake for 3 minutes more.

For frosting, combine brown sugar, water, and chocolate. Boil for 3 minutes; remove from burner. Add butter, 2 tablespoons vanilla, and powdered sugar. Spread over marshmallows and let cool. Cut into squares.

Strawberry Crunch Cake

2 c flour
2 tbsp whole-grain wheat flour
4 tsp baking powder
1/2 c sugar
3/4 tsp salt
3/4 c milk
2 eggs
1/2 tsp lemon extract
1 tsp vanilla
2 c fresh strawberries, sliced
1/2 c sugar
1/3 c sugar
1/3 c flour
2 tbsp whole-grain wheat flour
1/3 c butter, softened
1/4 tsp nutmeg
whipped cream

Combine first 9 ingredients and mix well. (Batter will be quite thick.) Spread in a greased 10-inch springform pan.

Sprinkle sliced strawberries and 1/2 cup sugar over top of batter.

In another bowl, combine 1/3 cup sugar, flours, butter, and nutmeg. Mix with a fork until crumbly; sprinkle over strawberries.

Bake at 425°F for 30-40 minutes. Serve warm with whipped cream.

S'Mores Torte

cooking spray
flour or graham cracker crumbs for dusting pan
1/4 lb unsalted butter
3 milk chocolate bars (1.55 oz ea), broken up
2/3 c sugar
3 eggs
1 tsp vanilla extract
2 c graham cracker crumbs
1 1/2 c mini marshmallows

Preheat oven to 350°F. Spray bottom and sides of an 8-inch layer pan with cooking spray. Line pan bottom with parchment or waxed paper, spray with more cooking spray, and dust with flour or graham cracker crumbs.

In a large heavy saucepan over medium heat, begin melting butter. When butter is half melted, add chocolate and stir until chocolate is half melted.

Remove from heat and stir until both are fully melted. Mix in sugar, eggs, vanilla, graham cracker crumbs, and marshmallows.

Pour and scrape batter into pan and bake until top is browned, edges are crusty, and only very center is still soft (about 30 minutes).

Cool in pan on a rack for 20 minutes. Run a knife around edge of the cake, cover with waxed paper and invert onto a plate.

Remove pan and peel off lining paper. Cover with a rack and invert again. Remove plate and waxed paper and cool about 15 minutes more.

Index